Positive Behavior Support for People With Developmental Disabilities

A Research Synthesis

By

Edward G. Carr, PhD
State University of New York at Stony Brook and
Developmental Disabilities Institute

Robert H. Horner, PhD
University of Oregon

Ann P. Turnbull, EdD
Janet G. Marquis, PhD
University of Kansas

Darlene Magito McLaughlin, MA
Michelle L. McAtee, MA
Christopher E. Smith, PhD
Kaarin Anderson Ryan, MA
State University of New York at Stony Brook

Michael B. Ruef, PhD
University of Kansas

Ajit Doolabh, MA
State University of New York at Stony Brook

David Braddock, PhD
Editor, Research Monographs and Books

American Association on Mental Retardation

Published by
American Association on Mental Retardation
444 North Capitol Street, NW, Suite 846
Washington, DC 20001-1512

The points of view herein are those of the authors and do not necessarily represent the official policy or opinion of the American Association on Mental Retardation. Publication does not imply endorsement by the editor, the Association, or its individual members.

Printed in the United States of America.

Library of Congress Cataloging-in-Publication Data
Positive behavior support for people with developmental disabilities:
a research synthesis/by Edward G. Carr...[et. al.].
p. cm.
Includes bibliographical references.
ISBN 0-940898-60-8
1. Mentally handicapped—Behavior modification.
I. Carr, Edward G., 1947-
RC451.4.M47P67   1999
616.85'884—dc21   99-22505
                                                                CIP

Preparation of this manuscript was supported in part by Grant #H023E50001 from the Office of Special Education Programs, "Synthesizing and Communicating a Professional Knowledge Base on Positive Behavioral Support." The opinions expressed herein do not necessarily reflect those of the U.S. Department of Education.

Portions of this paper were presented at the annual meeting of the American Association on Mental Retardation, New York, May 1997.

TABLE OF CONTENTS

TABLES

FIGURES

ACKNOWLEDGMENTS

We thank Doug Anderson, Mike Cataldo, Harris Cooper, Esther Lerner, Denise Poston, Wayne Sailor, Martha Snell, and Mark Wolery for their helpful comments. We especially thank Ellen Schiller of the Office of Special Education Programs for her ongoing support and feedback.

Address all correspondence to Edward Carr, Dept. of Psychology, State University of New York, Stony Brook, NY 11794-2500.

FOREWORD

Positive Behavioral Support and Applied Behavior Analysis

Todd R. Risley, PhD

University of Alaska

The dimensions of Applied Behavior Analysis were developed by Montrose Wolf and his colleagues in a remarkable series of exploratory studies, across a variety of children and problems, at the University of Washington in 1962–64. Those studies modeled how to arrange interventions in clinics, playgrounds, classrooms, and homes. They demonstrated the speed and power to change behavior of procedures based on the principles of behavior as delineated by B. F. Skinner. And they developed measurement tactics and experimental design variations to fit each new real-world condition and problem behavior encountered (see Risley, 1997 for a listing of these studies). It is important to note the three unprecedented and audacious features of those pioneering studies: 1) deliberate interventions in the daily lives of people; 2) fast and large behavior change; and 3) scientific documentation of field research. With the institution of the Journal of Applied Behavior Analysis in 1968, each of these features has been narrowed and codified across succeeding generations of researchers.

Thirty years later this monograph— *"Positive Behavior Support for People With Developmental Disabilities: A Research Synthesis"*—has reviewed the last 10 years of a major branch of Applied Behavior Analysis and has recommended some changes in direction. Their review is carefully designed and conducted—this is not biased assertion, but an objective meta-analysis with well defined, reliable variables. (Its clarity and sophistication are such that I regard it as a model of logic and methodology for Graduate research courses.) Their findings are presented with caution—this is not polemic or salesmanship, but reasoned consideration. (In fact, I think it understates the evidence favoring Positive Behavioral Support strategies.) Their recommendations are wise and practical—this is not pie-in-the-sky wishful thinking but a useful guide to the next generation of research, service, and policy. (I am gratified by this evidence of wisdom, leadership, and cooperation in the third and fourth generations of applied behavioral researchers.)

In their recommendations they state that we need a new applied science. Thirty-five years ago Montrose Wolf and a few others said the same—and proceeded to found Applied Behavior Analysis with only a little experience from which to deduce its characteristics. In contrast, these 10 authors represent scores of other researchers and have examined hundreds of studies. Their basis for recommending the dimensions of future Positive Behavioral Support is simply a conservative extrapolation of information.

Some of their recommendations to researchers suggest only a more systematic approach to things currently done. "Consumer needs" and "Participatory Action Research" is an (admittedly large) extension in the effort and timing of "Social Validity." If functional assessment is to have ecological validity it must be done throughout life, and therefore, "hypotheses" of antecedent and consequence functions can often be tested by close monitoring during interventions. Goals of life improvement and long-term benefits are now frequently (if poorly) addressed in anecdotal reports supplementing primary data.

However, there are fundamental attributes of Applied Behavior Analysis with which their recommendations conflict: procedural specificity, and demonstration of causality. Are these attributes of Applied Behavior Analysis fundamental to the advancement of knowledge? Perhaps not as much as we assume.

The recommendations for multicomponent interventions, individually adapted to circumstances and revised over time, is contrary to the goals of specifiable treatment "packages" or "manualized" treatments or "model" treatment programs common in Applied Behavior Analysis. Some specificity of intervention is, of course, desirable but to what use has it been put in 30 years of behavioral research?

This monograph, itself, is a most rare example of careful comparison of procedures across studies. More commonly we have quite similar procedures with different "proprietary" labels, and common labels masking large differences between intervention programs. Other areas of science and technology that have different customs for analyzing procedures across researchers should be examined for guidance; as should field trial protocols which specify treatments by their adherence to a set of decision rules rather than a set of fixed procedures.

The recommendations for larger interventions, goals, and measures cannot be met while adhering to high requirements of experimental manipulation. Despite occasional articles demonstrating or advocating the usefulness of group designs, correlations, naturalistic observations, and case studies in the *Journal of Applied Behavior Analysis*, demonstrations of causality over time have remained the standard for participation in Applied Behavior Analysis. It is this doctrine that most biases applied behavior analysis research toward more manageable contexts and problems. The demonstration of causality between independent and dependent variables through repeated manipulation of independent variables across time defined the Experimental Analysis of Behavior. The founders of Applied Behavior Analysis were active participants in the Experimental Analysis of Behavior journal and meetings. They never considered any other research logic. Some of the founders went so far as to *define* Applied Behavior Analysis *as* the use of single-subject time-series designs. Others disagreed and considered any research design to be simply a tool, to be chosen and used when needed.

It is clear that Positive Behavioral Support researchers need to use other tools in addition to experimental manipulations. Will Applied Behavior Analysis accommodate this, or will there become two distinct groups—one, allied to the Experimental Analysis of Behavior, and the other, dedicated to empirical problem-solving? It should be noted that empirical problem solving was the original impetus for the studies on which Applied Behavior Analysis was founded: problems were addressed as they presented themselves; measurement and research design considerations were overlaid to achieve the best information the circumstances allowed; the resulting publications were carefully considered reports of the problem-solving process, with due attention to threats to internal and external validity—not experiments proving a point. A healthy dose of Donald Campbell's consideration of problem-solving research (1957) and reforms as experiments (1969) would help the enterprise of Positive Behavioral Support pursue the recommendations proposed in this monograph and to return to the roots of Applied Behavior Analysis.

Campbell, D. T. (1957). Factors relevant to the validity of experiments in social settings. *Psychological Bulletin, 54*, 297-312.

Campbell, D. T. (1969). Reforms as experiments. *American Psychologist, 24*, 409-29.

Risley, T. R. (1997). Montrose M. Wolf: The origin of the dimensions of Applied Behavior Analysis, *Journal of Applied Behavior Analysis, 30*, 377-381.

FOREWORD

Madeleine Will, Former Assistant Secretary, OSERS

U.S. Department of Education

There are occasions when science confirms aspirations, when research justifies conviction. The analysis by Carr et al. is one of those.

It is a matter of record that during the time when I served as Assistant Secretary of Education, Office of Special Education and Rehabilitative Services (1983-1989), professionals, parents of children and adults with disabilities, self-advocates, and policy makers were locked in fierce debate concerning four matters on which I had chosen to take a leadership role: (a) inclusion of students with disabilities in regular education, (b) transition of students with disabilities from high school to work, (c) withholding or withdrawal of efficacious medical treatment from newborns who had obvious disabilities, and (d) the use of aversive behavioral interventions with children and adults with disabilities. In each of these issues policy decisions were made based on both technology and hope, on science and aspiration. In each case there was a capacity to do the right thing. More than that, there was a hope shared by myself and many others, that policy eventually would dignify the lives of people with disabilities by granting them new rights. This was especially true in the area of behavior support.

As I read the present monograph on Positive Behavior Support I could not help but recall the focus of our policy struggle in the late 1980s. Our efforts to match our aspirations with existing science were hindered, as is often the case, by the absence of science about the use of positive behavioral interventions. The monograph you hold before you is in many ways the document we wanted a decade ago. Here is a careful analysis documenting that positive behavioral procedures can produce important change in the behavior and lives of people with disabilities. Positive interventions can be effective.

Simply put: the monograph objectively reviews the published research on positive behavioral interventions and draws conclusions from this database. The organization and presentation of the published research is of special importance because it allows each reader to consider the conclusions in light of their personal interpretation of the data.

What I myself take from this review is that positive behavioral interventions are indeed beneficial; that they complement other practices that are now codified into policy (inclusion, transition to real work, and access to medical treatment); and that positive interventions are justified now on scientific grounds, just as some of us thought, long ago and still, that they are commanded on humane, moral, and constitutional grounds. Here, at last, is the proof positive of their efficacy. My son, Jonathan Will, and many other citizens with disabilities now have available to them (should they need it) a promising science that it was my privilege to stimulate and support. In a very practical way this monograph defines the science that confirms our aspiration; the research that justifies our convictions.

OVERVIEW

This monograph was prepared in response to a request from the United States Department of Education, Office of Special Education Programs, for a review of the literature on positive behavior support that provided (a) a definition of the approach, (b) an analysis of the database, (c) a delineation of gaps in our knowledge, and (d) suggestions for future directions. Because of the scope and complexity of the positive behavior support approach, it will be useful to begin with an overview of the main content areas of our monograph.

Positive behavior support (PBS) is an approach for dealing with problem behavior that focuses on the remediation of deficient contexts (i.e., environmental conditions and/or behavioral repertoires) that by functional assessment are documented to be the source of the problem. The research published on PBS between 1985 and 1996 was reviewed with respect to four categories of variables: demographics, assessment practices, intervention strategies, and outcomes.

The data derived from examining these four categories of variables were analyzed to answer five questions: (a) How widely applicable is PBS? (b) In what ways is the field evolving? (c) How effective is PBS? (d) What factors modulate the effectiveness of PBS? (e) How responsive is the PBS literature to the needs of consumers?

Results indicated that (a) PBS is widely applicable to people with serious problem behavior; (b) the field is growing rapidly overall, but especially in the use of assessment and in interventions that focus on correcting environmental deficiencies; (c) using stringent criteria of success, PBS is effective in reducing problem behavior in one half to two thirds of the cases; (d) success rates nearly double when intervention is based on a prior functional assessment; and (e) consumer needs that emphasize comprehensive lifestyle support, long-term change, practicality and relevance, and direct support for the consumers themselves are inadequately addressed by the research base.

Recommendations are made for bridging the research-to-practice gap in the areas of research priorities, service provision, social policy, and governmental action.

CHAPTER 1
INTRODUCTION

A new era of behavioral support is emerging. It is building from the careful, rigorous science of the past three decades and the practical demands of families, teachers, and clinicians. The new approach, called positive behavioral support (Koegel, Koegel, & Dunlap, 1996), is evolving rapidly as new information and challenges arise. The volume of recent empirical work suggests the need for a synthesis of the current research literature. The purpose of this research synthesis is to (a) define positive behavioral support, (b) provide a systematic analysis of the existing research database with respect to positive behavioral support, (c) compare that database with current clinical needs in the field, and (d) suggest future directions for research, practice, and policy. Our focus is on the application of behavioral support for people with developmental disabilities and autism.

We provide an introduction to the research synthesis by presenting (a) a brief overview and definition of positive behavior support, (b) the rationale for the present research synthesis of positive behavior support, (c) the research questions posed, and (d) the structure of the research synthesis.

Positive Behavioral Support: Overview and Definition

Problem behaviors such as aggression, self-injury, tantrums, and property destruction have long been barriers to successful education, socialization, employment, and community adaptation (Meyer, Peck, & Brown, 1991; Scheerenberger, 1990; White, Lakin, Bruininks, & Li, 1991). The goal of positive behavior support (PBS) is to apply behavioral principles in the community in order to reduce problem behaviors and build appropriate behaviors that result in durable change and a rich lifestyle. The foundation of PBS lies in early efforts to apply principles of behavior to improve the lives of children with severe problem behaviors (Bijou & Baer, 1961; Bijou, Peterson, & Ault, 1968; Browning & Stover, 1971). The lawful relationships between behavior and environment were applied to people with real problems. The results were encouraging and led to the development in the 1960s and 1970s of an array of intervention procedures (Barrett, 1986; Foxx, 1982; Kazdin, 1980). Each of these procedures proved successful at reducing problem behaviors in some situations and unsuccessful in others.

The need to improve the application of intervention procedures led to a renewed appreciation for the earlier call to organize interventions based on a careful functional assessment of the problem behavior (Baer, Wolf, & Risley, 1968; Bijou et al., 1968). Beginning in the late 1970s (Carr, 1977) and continuing through today, the concept of functional assessment has been transformed into a practical technology for guiding the development of behavioral interventions (Bailey & Pyles, 1989; Gardner & Sovner, 1994; O'Neill, Horner, Albin, Storey, & Sprague, 1997a & b; Reichle & Wacker, 1993).

A central result has been an expansion of interventions beyond those based on consequence manipulations to include (a) altering the environment before problem behaviors occur, and (b) teaching appropriate behaviors as an effective strategy for reducing unwanted behaviors. Behavioral support is becoming less a process of selecting *an* intervention, and more the construction of a comprehensive set of procedures that include change of the environment to make problem behaviors irrelevant, instruction on appropriate behaviors that makes the problem behavior inefficient, and manipulation of consequences to ensure that appropriate behaviors are more consistently and powerfully reinforced than are problem behaviors. As the structure of behavioral support expands, so does recognition that a complete technology will also require attention to those interacting variables in a setting/system that affect the implementation of effective procedures (Sailor, 1996; Taylor-Greene et al., 1997).

As effective approaches to behavioral support emerged, expectations for the outcomes and acceptability of the technology were redefined. The initial focus of behavioral interventions was on simple reduction of problem behaviors. As this proved possible, yet insufficient, expectations changed. Through reexamination of original assumptions (Baer et al., 1968) and attention to the messages provided by real-world users of the technology, investigators expanded functional assessment technology and the expectations for behavioral interventions were redefined. Effective behavioral support needed not only to reduce problem behaviors, but also to build prosocial behavior, document durable change, generalize across the full range of situations an individual encountered, and produce access to a rich lifestyle.

This is the key concept that defines PBS: To remediate problem behavior, it is necessary first to remediate deficient contexts. There are two kinds of deficiencies: those relating to environmental conditions, and those relating to behavior repertoires. Environmental conditions are deficient to the extent that they involve lack of choice, inadequate teaching strategies, minimal access to engaging materials and activities, poorly selected daily routines, and a host of other proximal and distal antecedent stimuli related to the previous factors. Behavior repertoires are deficient to the extent that communication skills, self-management, social skills, and other constructive behaviors are inadequately developed or absent. (The constituent elements relating to the two kinds of deficiencies just summarized are defined at length in Chapter 2, under the subhead Intervention Strategies.) Recently there has been much discussion concerning the strong association between these two types of deficiencies and the display of problem behavior; many have concluded that problem behavior can be effectively addressed by focusing on the assessment and remediation of context (Emerson, McGill, & Mansell, 1994; Koegel et al., 1996; Luiselli & Cameron, 1998; Lutzker & Campbell, 1994; Reichle & Wacker, 1993).

As noted, the primary focus of the field has not always been on context per se. For many years, researchers and clinicians alike emphasized strategies that concentrated on the problem behavior itself (e.g., aggression, self-injury, and property destruction), rather than on deficiencies such as poor environmental conditions or a lack of functional skills.

This emphasis led to the development of a wide variety of reactive (often punitive) interventions designed to suppress or eliminate the problem behavior directly (Bucher & Lovaas, 1968; Cataldo, 1991; Harris & Ersner-Hershfield, 1978; Matson & DiLorenzo, 1984). The relative merits of reactive versus contextually based interventions have been hotly debated in the literature (Guess, Helmstetter, Turnbull, & Knowlton, 1987; Repp & Singh, 1990). Yet people on all sides of this debate have always acknowledged that the ultimate goal is not simply the reduction of problem behavior, but rather improving people's lives. There is now widespread appreciation of the fact that the negative sequelae of problem behavior include not only physical danger to self and others, but also educational segregation, limited employment opportunities, rejection by members of the community, separation from home and family, and, finally, social ostracism and a life without friendship (National Institutes of Health, 1991). Clearly, behavioral technology must now become more comprehensive in scope and more cognizant of the role of the larger systems (e.g., family, school, employment, and funding) that influence the practicality of effective behavioral support (Sailor, 1996). Consideration of these larger issues has prompted interest in the kinds of environmental and behavioral context variables that are the essential characteristics of PBS.

It may be worthwhile at this point to further distinguish PBS from other contemporary approaches. The two most substantive and frequently employed alternatives to PBS are the use of pharmacotherapy (medication) and aversive procedures. As noted previously, the main focus of aversive procedures is the elimination, through punishment, of problem behavior. Such procedures are fundamentally and by definition reactive in nature. They are not employed until the problem behavior occurs. In contrast, PBS is proactive in nature. It is an attempt to remediate environmental and behavioral deficiencies so as to prevent future occurrences of the problem behavior. In sum, using aversive procedures conforms best to a crisis management paradigm; using PBS conforms best to a prevention paradigm. A detailed analysis of the aversives literature is ably presented elsewhere (Cataldo, 1991).

The second non-PBS strategy, medication, involves the use of one or more drugs to suppress problem behavior. Often the drugs are administered over a long period of time, to address hypothesized or identified biochemical aberrations thought to underlie problem behavior. In this case, the use of medication conforms to a preventive paradigm, because the successful use of medication would block the occurrence of future episodes of problem behavior. Sophisticated analyses of the voluminous and complex pharmacotherapy literature are also available elsewhere (Reiss & Aman, 1998; Schaal & Hackenberg, 1994; Schroeder & Tessel, 1994; Thompson, Hackenberg, & Schaal, 1991). There is an obvious distinction between PBS and pharmacotherapy: Whereas the former focuses on the role of environmental factors in assessing and remediating problem behavior, the latter focuses on the role of biochemical factors.

Some people question the advisability of comparing PBS with medication and the use of aversives. Our position, articulated in detail later, is that there are many good reviews of non-PBS strategies but a dearth of reviews concerning the unique contributions of PBS per se.

Therefore, we will focus our review on PBS alone. More important, making comparisons among these approaches would implicitly support what we believe is a false assumption: that one must always choose among the three approaches because only one can be ascendant. Clinical experience would seem to contradict this assumption. For example, for many years, it has been considered a best practice to accompany the use of aversives with a detailed educational and social support plan that embodies the major features of PBS (Carr & Lovaas, 1983; Foxx, 1982, 1990; Foxx, Bittle, & Faw, 1989). Likewise, the literature on dual diagnosis indicates a potentially important role for medication. Specifically, some people with developmental disabilities may receive a secondary diagnosis such as depression, anxiety, bipolar disorder, or obsessive-compulsive disorder (Bodfish & Madison, 1993; Lowry & Sovner, 1992; Ratey, Sovner, Parks, & Rogentine, 1991; Reiss & Rojahn, 1993). An emerging literature suggests that medication given to alleviate the symptoms associated with the secondary diagnosis may help reduce problem behavior (e.g., Bodfish & Madison, 1993; Sovner, 1989). As yet, there is no definitive research demonstrating a causal link between obsessive-compulsive disorder, for example, and problem behavior. Nonetheless, the empirical work on dual diagnosis sounds a cautionary note in that practitioners must consider the possibility that PBS alone might prove insufficient for dealing with individuals carrying diagnostic labels beyond developmental disabilities per se. Similarly, medication alone might prove insufficient for improving an individual's lifestyle, one of the stated goals of PBS.

In sum, the three approaches for dealing with problem behavior do not exist independently of one another in practice. As yet, however, there is no well-developed research literature that explores, systematically, how the approaches interrelate.

Need for a Review of Positive Behavior Support

To date, there have been few synthesis reviews focused on PBS per se. This approach did not gain momentum until the mid-to-late 1980s, after which there was an explosive growth in the number of research studies, conceptual papers, and intervention manuals related to PBS (Carr et al., 1994; Donnellan, LaVigna, Negri-Shoultz, & Fassbender, 1988; Durand, 1990; Evans & Meyer, 1985; Horner, Dunlap et al., 1990; LaVigna & Donnellan, 1986; Meyer & Evans, 1989; Smith, 1990). There have been many excellent reviews dealing with the general issue of remediating problem behavior. Typically, however, reviewers combined the analysis of PBS with the analysis of other approaches that differ from PBS, or they reviewed only a subset of PBS procedures (Didden, Duker, & Korzilius, 1997; Lancioni & Hoogeveen, 1990; Lennox, Miltenberger, Spengler, & Erfanian, 1988; Matson & Taras, 1989; O'Brien & Repp, 1990; Vollmer & Iwata, 1992). Consequently, previous reviews did not analyze, in depth, the unique contributions made by PBS per se.

The dearth of synthesis reviews related to PBS was one reason for the National Institutes of Health commissioning a Consensus Development Conference in 1989 to deal with the issue of destructive behavior. One product of that conference was a synthesis review of PBS based on the literature that existed through 1989 (Carr, Robinson, Taylor, & Carlson, 1990). Shortly thereafter a second analysis appeared reviewing the literature from 1976 to 1987 (Scotti, Evans, Meyer, & Walker, 1991). This analysis considered a number of issues relevant to PBS but devoted considerable coverage to non-PBS strategies as well. Finally, a recent review (Scotti, Ujcich, Weigle, Holland, & Kirk, 1996) analyzed intervention practices (but not outcomes) from 1988 to 1992 and extended the initial Scotti et al. (1991) review. Again, however, the analysis included non-PBS strategies. In sum, the absence, since 1989, of a synthesis that focuses exclusively on PBS provided an important justification for undertaking the present review.

Traditionally reviews have emphasized issues of special interest to researchers: population demographics, experimental design considerations, assessment strategies, and measures of comparative intervention effectiveness. But as the field has matured, there has been greater appreciation for the perspectives of nonresearchers (consumers). In this review, we use the term *consumers* to include people with disabilities, their teachers, their friends, members of their families, administrators, and policy makers. The literature suggests that although PBS has made a major contribution in dealing with the issue of problem behavior, a considerable gap exists between the needs and interests of researchers and nonresearcher consumers (Billingsley & Cross, 1991; Dunlap, Robbins, & Darrow, 1994; Haring, 1996; Horner, Diemer, & Brazeau, 1992; Sailor, 1996; Turnbull & Turnbull, 1996). Considering this gap, we set out to determine how far the literature has come

in addressing this gap and, by implication, what must be done next. This objective could be achieved only through a careful analysis of those parts of the PBS literature that, explicitly or implicitly, bear on the perspectives of nonresearchers. The relative absence of this type of analysis from previous reviews was another reason to examine the PBS literature as it has evolved to date.

Research Questions Posed: Contributions of the Review

In this section, we outline the major research questions posed in the review and the kinds of information derived from answering them. First, however, it is necessary to elaborate further on the defining characteristics of PBS so they can be systematically related to the key research questions.

Elaboration of Defining Characteristics of PBS

From the standpoint of the independent variable, the PBS approach refers to those interventions that involve altering deficient environmental conditions (e.g., activity patterns, choice options, prompting procedures) and/or deficient behavior repertoires (e.g., communication, self-management, social skills). The alteration of *environmental conditions* can be achieved by modifying proximal stimuli (e.g., curriculum materials, prompts) or distal stimuli (e.g., rearranging the sequence of daily life routines). Because all such strategies focus on assessing and manipulating stimuli, we will refer to these strategies as stimulus-based interventions. The alteration of *behavior repertoires* can be achieved by modifying

7

socially appropriate, functional behaviors that are currently inadequately developed or absent (e.g., communication, job skills, social skills, independent living skills, self-management behavior). Because all strategies that increase the probability of such behaviors invariably involve a systematic and targeted application of reinforcement, we refer to these strategies as reinforcement-based intervention. The various parameters of stimulus-based and reinforcement-based interventions define the core of PBS with respect to the independent variables.

The remediation of deficient contexts also helps to define the PBS approach with respect to dependent variables: (a) increased positive behavior, (b) improved lifestyle, and (c) decreased problem behavior. Specifically, as noted, stimulus- and reinforcement-based interventions are both designed to increase the probability that socially appropriate, functional behaviors (i.e., positive behaviors) will occur. For example, improvements made in instructional procedures (a stimulus-based strategy) may increase correct academic responding (a positive behavior); that is, the revised instructional procedures contain discriminative stimuli that evoke correct academic responding at a higher rate. Likewise, strengthening communicative skills (a reinforcement-based strategy) may increase a variety of positive, constructive behaviors such as making requests, providing information, and protesting unwanted interactions. Increases in the probability of functional positive behaviors (whether produced by stimulus- or reinforcement-based interventions) can also potentially facilitate widespread changes in an individual's life situation, bringing about improvements in social, vocational, and educational status (i.e., lifestyle change). Finally, improvements in environmental conditions and repertoires of positive behavior can produce, as a side effect, decreases in problem behavior. In sum, increases in positive behavior, lifestyle change, and subsequent decreases in problem behavior define the core of PBS with respect to the dependent variables (Horner, Dunlap et al., 1990).

Research Questions

Having defined PBS in terms of its core independent and dependent variables, we can now pose the research questions that provide the structure for this review.

How Widely Applicable Is PBS?

The answer to this question will contribute information concerning whether PBS interventions are applicable across gender, a broad age range, diagnosis, level of retardation, and type of problem behavior. Also, the answer will make clear who implements PBS (intervention agent) and where it takes place (intervention setting).

In What Ways Is the Field Evolving?

The answer to this question will contribute information concerning the trends that have taken place over the 12-year period covered by the synthesis. These trends involve a consideration of changes across time in the volume of literature published as well as the types of interventions used, problem behaviors treated, assessments carried out, factors identified as maintaining the problem behavior, type of systems change, intervention agents and settings involved (ecological validity), breadth of intervention effects, and judgments of outcome and social validity made by significant others (e.g., consumers such as parents, teachers, job coaches). The analysis of trends also provides information as to whether the field as a whole is progressing toward a more widespread adoption of what are regarded as best practices.

How Effective Is PBS?

Answers to this question provide critical information used to compare the effectiveness of the entire category of stimulus-based intervention with the entire category of reinforcement-based intervention. We also present information concerning changes in effectiveness when the categories are combined with one another and with non-PBS strategies that are frequently a part of a multicomponent approach to intervention.

What Factors Modulate the Effectiveness of PBS?

Answers to this question provide information concerning how demographic, assessment, systems change, and ecological validity variables affect outcomes, that is, how these variables modulate the effectiveness of PBS-based intervention.

How Responsive Is the PBS Literature to the Needs of Consumers (Nonresearchers)?

Given that this question is typically not included in a research synthesis, we first discuss the rationale for its inclusion. The gap between the knowledge produced by research and the needs of consumers of research has prompted increasing national concern (Bruyère, 1993; Carnine, 1997; Fuchs & Fuchs, 1990; Hess & Mullen, 1995; Hoshmand & Polkinghorne, 1992; Huberman, 1990; Kaufman, Schiller, Birman, & Coutinho, 1993; Lather, 1986; Lloyd, Weintraub, & Safer, 1997). A

number of factors converge, related to PBS, to escalate this national concern: (a) trends of deinstitutionalization and community inclusion for students with severe disabilities (Braddock, Hemp, Fujiura, Bachelder, & Mitchell, 1990), (b) the mandate of the Vocational Rehabilitation Act to conduct consumer-responsive research (S. Rep. No. 102-357, 1992), and (c) the 1997 Amendments to the Individuals With Disabilities Education Act that strongly emphasize requirements for functional behavior assessment and behavioral intervention in dealing with issues pertaining to student discipline (Individuals With Disabilities Education Act, 1997).

Answers to the question related to the responsiveness of the PBS literature contribute information concerning the degree to which the research literature is usable and accessible from consumers' perspectives (Carnine, 1997). We identify and examine in light of the database priority concerns in the consumer literature. The gap between consumer concerns and the database contribute heuristic information concerning the formulation of a future research agenda and the delineation of roles related to research translation, dissemination, and use.

The Structure of the Research Synthesis

In Chapter 2, "Methods," we (a) operationally define the demographic, assessment, intervention, and outcome variables pertinent to the database, (b) explicate literature search strategies and eligibility (inclusion/exclusion) criteria, and (c) describe data collection and measurement methods.

Chapter 3, "Results," is structured around the first four research questions. It begins with summary descriptive statistics on the demographic variables that characterize the literature included, thereby clarifying whether PBS is widely applicable across various demographic characteristics, problem behaviors, and intervention agents and settings. This section is followed by a presentation of data dealing with trends across time. Then we present data on intervention effectiveness, followed by data on variables that modulate effectiveness.

In Chapter 4, "Discussion," we first deal with the issue of potential biases in the literature retrieved. Then we develop a number of generalizations that can be inferred from the database on demographics, assessment, interventions, and outcomes. Within this chapter, we discuss the impact of the results on assessment and intervention practices. The last section outlines where the major gaps in knowledge are and offers a plan for addressing these gaps. This section draws on the database to address the final research question, namely, how responsive the PBS literature has been to the needs of consumers (nonresearchers).

In the final two chapters of the review, we summarize the major findings and provide a list of recommendations for advancing the field of PBS.

CHAPTER 2
METHODS

In this chapter, we (a) provide operational definitions of the four categories of variables, (b) explicate the literature search and eligibility criteria, and (c) describe the data collection methods.

Operational Definitions

Each article identified was scored with respect to four categories of variables: (a) demographics, (b) assessment practices, (c) intervention strategies, and (d) outcome measures.

Demographics

The following demographic variables were scored: (a) the year in which the article was published (1985-1996); those articles listed as being *in press* at the time of the review were assigned to the year 1996, for reasons explained later in the section on eligibility criteria; (b) gender of participants (male or female); (c) diagnosis (mental retardation; autism/pervasive developmental disability; mental retardation + autism/ pervasive developmental disability; mental retardation and/or autism/ pervasive developmental disability + other [e.g., anxiety disorder, motor skills disorder, tic disorder, etc.]); (d) age (age in years rounded to the nearest whole number); (e) level of mental retardation (profound, severe, moderate, mild); (f) type of problem behavior (aggression, self-injurious behavior, property destruction, tantrums).

Assessment Practices

Assessment practices are the methods practitioners and researchers use to determine (a) classes of problem behavior, (b) antecedents that occasion and do not occasion problem behavior, and (c) variables responsible for maintaining problem behavior. These maintaining variables are often referred to as the function, purpose, goal, intent, reinforcers, or motivation of problem behavior, terms that are roughly synonymous (Carr, 1993; Lee, 1988; Skinner, 1974).

The objective of assessment is to generate information that can be used to guide the selection and development of intervention strategies.

There are three categories of assessment: indirect observation (sometimes referred to as informal observation), direct observation (sometimes referred to as formal observation), and functional analysis (Lennox & Miltenberger, 1989; O'Neill et al., 1997a & b; Sturmey, 1994). Indirect or informal observation involves assessment strategies in which information about problem behavior (B), its antecedents (A), and consequences (C) are gathered indirectly (via informants) through the use of interviews (e.g., Carr et al., 1994; O'Neill et al., 1997 a & b), questionnaires (e.g, Durand & Crimmins, 1992), rating scales (Aman, Singh, Stewart, & Field, 1985), setting-event inventories that focus on broad contextual variables such as daily schedules and health status (e.g., Gardner & Sovner, 1994; O'Neill et al., 1997a & b), or anecdotal observations. Direct or formal observation involves direct measurement through the use of A-B-C data sheets (e.g., Bijou et al., 1968), scatterplots that document temporal correlations between problem behavior and specific situations (Touchette,

MacDonald, & Langer, 1985), and time sampling and/or frequency counts (e.g., Lalli, Browder, Mace, & Brown, 1993; O'Neill et al., 1997a & b). Functional analysis involves the systematic (experimental) manipulation of the variables thought to control problem behavior and is carried out to test hypotheses about motivation (Carr, 1994). Assessments may be repeated over time if circumstances change, warranting further investigation of motivational hypotheses (Mace, 1994; Vollmer, Marcus, & LeBlanc, 1994).

The product of these assessments is a statement concerning the problem behavior, controlling antecedents, and maintaining consequences (motivation). There are four commonly identified motivational categories: attention, escape, tangibles/activities, and sensory reinforcement (Carr, 1977; Iwata, Dorsey, Slifer, Bauman, & Richman, 1982; Wiesler, Hanson, Chamberlain, & Thompson, 1985). Sometimes problem behavior (a) functions to secure *attention,* nurturance, and comfort from others (Carr & McDowell, 1980; Lovaas, Freitag, Gold, & Kassorla, 1965; Martin & Foxx, 1973); (b) helps individuals *escape* or avoid difficult, boring, or arduous tasks and other aversive situations (Carr & Newsom, 1985; Carr, Newsom, & Binkoff, 1976, 1980; Patterson, 1982); (c) helps provide the individual with *access to desirable tangible items* and preferred activities (Derby et al., 1992; Durand & Crimmins, 1988); or (d) generates *sensory reinforcement* in the form of visual, auditory, tactile, and even gustatory stimulation (Favell, McGimsey, & Schell, 1982; Rincover, Cook, Peoples, & Packard, 1979). A given problem behavior may have more than one function (Day, Horner, & O'Neill, 1994; Haring & Kennedy, 1990; Iwata et al., 1982). It

should be noted that other sources of motivation, such as social avoidance (Taylor & Carr, 1992), have been identified. Indeed, it has been hypothesized that there may be as many as 16 different motives for problem behavior (Reiss & Havercamp, 1997). However, the empirical base demonstrating these additional sources of motivation is, as yet, too small for review purposes.

Summary

Using the terms just delineated, we scored those aspects of assessment practices that corresponded to the following questions: (a) Was there an assessment of function (yes/no)? (b) What assessment strategy was used (informal observation, formal direct observation, functional analysis)? (c) What functions were identified (attention, escape, tangibles/activities, sensory)? (d) Was the assessment repeated over time? (e) Was the assessment information subsequently used to design an intervention?

Intervention Strategies

Within the theme of intervention strategies, we scored articles with respect to (a) intervention category, (b) systems change, and (c) ecological validity.

Intervention Categories

As noted previously, there are two categories of PBS intervention: those designed to make positive behavior more probable by (a) remediating deficient environmental conditions (stimulus-based intervention) and (b) remediating deficient behavior repertoires (reinforcement-based intervention). The literature reviewed demonstrated a large number of variations associated with each category of intervention but, typically, only a small number of cases associated with any particular variation. To further clarify the defining properties of the two generic categories that served as the basis for our data coding, we delineate here the characteristics of some of the many variations identified in the literature.

Stimulus-Based Intervention

From a functional standpoint, deficient environments provide too few stimuli that support positive behavior and too many that support problem behavior. Thus, one functional theme unites all variations in this category: Environmental repair is attempted through the manipulation of stimuli that are proximal and distal to the behaviors of interest. The structural nuances that distinguish each variation are less important than the functional utility shared by all in modifying the environment to promote positive behavior. To illustrate the breadth of stimulus-based intervention, we here describe some of the more salient variations noted in the literature.

Interspersal training. In the literature this strategy is variously referred to as interspersal training (Horner, Day, Sprague, O'Brien, & Heathfield, 1991), behavioral momentum (Mace, Hock, et al., 1988), pretask requesting (Singer, Singer, & Horner, 1987), task variation (Dunlap & Koegel, 1980; Winterling, Dunlap, & O'Neill, 1987), and embedding (Carr et al., 1976). The essence of these procedures is to present a stimulus (e.g., a difficult task demand such as "clean up your toys") known to be discriminative for problem behavior (e.g., aggression) within the context of stimuli (e.g., easy demands such as "give me a hug") known to be discriminative for nonproblem behavior (e.g., complying with the request to hug). These stimulus changes result in

the formerly problematic stimulus (i.e., "clean up your toys") now evoking cooperation rather than aggression.

Expansion of choice. This strategy involves presenting the individual with a number of choice stimuli (options) related to a wide variety of activities and/ or tasks, and permitting the individual to express a preference (choose) among the options. Research suggests that expanding choices can be an effective way to reduce problem behavior (Bannerman, Sheldon, Sherman, & Harchik, 1990; Dunlap, dePerczel et al., 1994; Dyer, Dunlap, & Winterling, 1990; Koegel, Dyer, & Bell, 1987; Vaughn & Horner, 1997).

Curricular modification. The essence of this strategy is to identify the aversive features of task stimuli that evoke escape-motivated problem behavior, and then to minimize or eliminate those features. Dunlap, Kern-Dunlap, Clarke, and Robbins (1991) demonstrated the efficacy of this procedure by altering features such as task length, task outcomes, and clarity of instructions, the modification of which was correlated with decreases in problem behavior.

Manipulation of setting events. Another intervention from the generic stimulus-based category involves the manipulation of setting events. Setting events are broad contextual variables (often involving distal stimuli) that alter the relationship between discriminative stimuli and responses (Bijou & Baer, 1961). Setting events include (a) physical factors such as environmental enrichment (Horner, 1980), (b) biological factors such as drugs (Thompson et al., 1991) and illness (Carr & Smith, 1995), and (c) social factors such as the presence versus absence of specific people (Touchette et al., 1985) and the sequencing of interpersonal activities (Brown,

1991). Setting events often serve as establishing operations (Michael, 1982), that is, as factors that momentarily change the reinforcing or aversive properties of response consequences, thereby influencing the probability of constructive behavior as well as problem behavior.

Reinforcement-Based Intervention

A deficient positive-behavior repertoire makes it difficult (or impossible) for an individual to meet his or her needs (i.e., access preferred reinforcers), which, in turn, increases the level of frustration (i.e., maximizes episodes of extinction), thereby leading to problem behavior; if an individual's current repertoire of nonproblem (positive) behavior is ineffective in gaining reinforcers but his or her problem behavior is effective, then problem behavior will become more probable. From a functional standpoint, the presence of positive behaviors compete with and/or make problem behavior unnecessary because the positive behaviors themselves provide alternative avenues for accessing valued reinforcers.

There are many variations of reinforcement-based interventions. One common theme unites all the variations: They target specific behaviors or classes of behaviors for consistent, systematic reinforcement.

By way of illustrating this broad generic category, we here describe several of the many variations of reinforcement-based interventions noted in the literature. Note that one procedure, differential reinforcement of other behavior (DRO), despite its name, is not an example of reinforcement-based intervention given the criteria we are using. DRO involves delivering reinforcement contingent on the nonoccurrence of the target problem behavior for a prespecified period of time

(Vollmer & Iwata, 1992). No positive behavior(s) is (are) explicitly targeted for reinforcement, which is why some researchers prefer to call the procedure "differential reinforcement of not responding" or "zero responding" (Poling & Ryan, 1982; Zeiler, 1970). Indeed, some have argued that the DRO procedure can be viewed as a form of punishment, because frequent display of problem behavior results in repeated omission of positive reinforcers, an aversive event (Rolider & Van Houten, 1990).

Functional communication training. This intervention involves teaching an individual a specific communicative response that serves the same function (functional equivalence) as the problem behavior it is intended to replace (Carr & Durand, 1985). In illustration, a functional analysis indicates that a young girl with autism becomes self-injurious in the presence of negative academic feedback because of a history of reinforcement for such behavior (i.e., self-injury results in termination of the putatively aversive instructional situation). Following the functional analysis, the teacher makes changes. She prompts the girl to request "help" in response to negative feedback (e.g., the teacher says, "No, that's not the right answer"; then the teacher provides a prompt, "Say, 'Help me, please'"). If the new communicative response is more efficient (Horner & Day, 1991) at terminating the aversive events associated with the task than self-injury (i.e., communication requires less effort to escape from the negative feedback than self-injurious behavior), then the problem behavior is likely to decrease (Bird, Dores, Moniz, & Robinson, 1989; Carr & Durand, 1985; Day, Rea, Schussler, Larsen, & Johnson, 1988; Durand & Carr, 1991, 1992; Wacker et al., 1990).

Self-management. Self-management involves any of three component skills: self-monitoring, self-evaluation, and self-reinforcement. Self-monitoring involves teaching an individual to discriminate appropriate versus inappropriate behaviors and to describe each of them (e.g., "I made my bed" versus "I bit my hand"). Self-evaluation consists of labeling a behavior as desirable versus undesirable. For example, after making the bed, the individual might be taught to say, "I did a good job." In contrast, after self-biting, the individual might be taught to say, "I didn't do a good job." Self-reinforcement consists of teaching the individual to deliver reinforcers (e.g., praise, tangibles) to him- or herself following a positive self-evaluation but not after a negative self-evaluation. In sum, the individual is taught to positively reinforce desirable response alternatives to the problem behavior. Studies suggest that instruction in self-management can reduce or eliminate disruptive, aggressive, and self-injurious behaviors (Gardner, Cole, Berry, & Nowinski, 1983; Koegel, Koegel, Hurley, & Frea, 1992).

Differential reinforcement of alternative behavior (DRA). This intervention involves reinforcing those behaviors that are topographically different from the targeted problem behavior. The new behaviors thus serve as alternatives to the problem behavior. In an early demonstration of DRA, Hall, Lund, and Jackson (1968) reinforced (with teacher attention) the "study" behavior of elementary school students, while applying extinction to their disruptive behavior. As the alternative (study) behaviors were strengthened, there was a concomitant decrease in problem behavior (disruption).

Non-PBS (Environmentally Based) Intervention

There were many instances in the literature in which PBS interventions were combined with non-PBS (environmentally based) interventions. These latter interventions were defined as those for which the primary goal was the reduction of problem behavior through the direct application of procedures reactive to the display of problem behavior. Of the many variations of non-PBS procedures, three are described that illustrate the reactive nature of non-PBS (in contrast to the proactive nature of PBS).

The first procedure, differential reinforcement of other behavior (DRO), has already been discussed. In brief, DRO, applied during a bout of problem behavior, involves delivering reinforcement contingent on the nonoccurrence of problem behavior for a prespecified period of time. A second procedure, extinction, involves withdrawing the reinforcer that maintains the problem behavior each time that the problem behavior occurs. The status of extinction as a non-PBS procedure is debatable. In a later section, we discuss the possibility, based on conceptual and pragmatic considerations, that extinction might also be viewed as a key aspect of PBS. A third procedure, timeout, involves the withdrawal of all positive reinforcement for a fixed time period following the occurrence of problem behavior. This procedure is considered a form of punishment.

Systems Change

PBS involves systems change, not just change in the individual who displays problem behavior. Both stimulus-based intervention and reinforcement-based intervention potentially result in changes in how other people respond to the person with disabilities and how the environment is organized. We examined these two aspects of systems change.

Behavior Change on the Part of Significant Others

We determined whether people other than the person with disabilities were required to alter aspects of their behavior as part of the intervention. In illustration, consider functional communication training. If an individual with disabilities was taught to request help in response to a difficult task, then the support person (e.g., a parent or teacher) would be expected to respond to the request by providing help; the support person was required to change his or her behavior in response to change in the behavior of the person with disabilities. If an investigator explicitly noted such a requirement, we scored this aspect of systems change as being present.

Broad Environmental Reorganization and Restructuring

We also determined whether broad reorganization and/or restructuring of the environment (Emerson et al., 1994) was reported as part of the intervention approach. These environmental variables included any variation of the following: systematic personnel changes; alterations in the scheduling of activities; provision of supported employment; provision of new, enriching community activities; provision of respite services; friendship facilitation; provision of additional staff; physical alteration of the home and/or school setting; addition (and/or removal) of individuals with disabilities to/from specific classrooms and/or group homes; and provision of choices all day long (i.e., not just in selected circumstances). If an investigator systematically included one

or more of the preceding variables as part of an intervention, this aspect of systems change was scored as being present.

Ecological Validity

PBS is not intended to be a laboratory-based demonstration or analog but, rather, a strategy for dealing with problem behavior in all pertinent natural contexts. We documented this aspect of PBS intervention by examining (a) who carried out the intervention (the intervention agent), (b) where the intervention took place (intervention setting), and (c) whether the intervention was implemented in all contexts in which problem behavior was noted to occur (all relevant contexts).

Intervention Agent

A distinction can be made between intervention agents who would normally be expected to be the primary support people/caregivers in a particular community setting (hereafter referred to as typical intervention agents) and those who would not normally be involved (hereafter referred to as atypical intervention agents). In the home setting, the typical intervention agent would be a parent or other close relative of a child or adolescent; in the school setting, a teacher; in a group home setting, direct care staff; in supported living, a housemate; and, in the workplace, a job coach or designated fellow employee. We defined all such individuals, in these and other relevant community settings, as typical intervention agents. In contrast, atypical intervention agents included psychologists, behavior specialists, researchers, and others who would not be expected to provide support on a day-to-day basis under normal circumstances.

In our synthesis, the involvement of

typical intervention agents reflects high ecological validity; the involvement of atypical agents reflects low validity.

Intervention Setting

A distinction can be made between living environments that are considered normative for an individual of a given age (hereafter referred to as typical settings), and those not considered normative (hereafter referred to as atypical settings). According to this criterion, typical settings include the home, integrated school, group home/own home, job site, neighborhood, and a variety of community settings (e.g., those related to recreational activities, shopping, eating, and entertainment). Using the same criterion, atypical settings include segregated schools, psychiatric wards/ hospitals, medical clinics, state institutions, and sheltered workshops. With respect to the concept of PBS, interventions taking place in typical settings reflect high ecological validity, while those taking place in atypical settings reflect low validity.

Intervention in All Relevant Contexts

Context has two dimensions: temporal and situational. For scoring purposes, the relevant context for carrying out an intervention for problem behavior included all the time periods for which the problem was reported to occur, and all the situations for which it was reported to occur. In illustration, a teacher might report that problem behavior occurred throughout the school day and across many different situations (e.g., during gym, lunch time, reading, group circle, dismissal, boarding the bus). An investigator might respond to the teacher's referral by removing the child from the classroom and conducting 20-minute intervention sessions in a special tutorial room. Because these sessions do not cover the entire time period or array of situations for which the teacher reported the presence of problem behavior, we scored the implemented intervention as not having occurred in all relevant contexts. In contrast, a teacher might report that problem behavior occurred exclusively during the 20-minute daily gym session because the motor activities involved were singularly aversive to the individual. To bring about improved behavior, an investigator might instruct the teacher, in the gym setting, to alter the curriculum during the 20-minute session. In this case, the intervention session covers the entire time period in the situation identified by the teacher. This intervention would be scored as having occurred in all relevant contexts.

Because PBS interventions are intended to deal with problem behavior whenever and wherever it naturally occurs, the first intervention described would reflect low ecological validity; the second would reflect high validity.

Summary

Using the terms just delineated, we scored those aspects of an intervention that corresponded to the following questions: (a) Was the intervention stimulus-based, reinforcement-based, non-PBS based (yes/no for each)? (b) Systems change: Did the intervention involve change on the part of significant others and/or broad environmental reorganization and restructuring (yes/no for each)? (c) Ecological validity: What type of intervention agent was involved (typical/ atypical)? What type of intervention setting was involved (typical/atypical)? Did intervention occur in all relevant contexts (yes/no)?

Outcome Measures

Because PBS involves the multidimensional remediation of deficient context, the outcomes of the approach are likewise multidimensional. We examined seven outcome measures: (a) positive behavior, (b) problem behavior, (c) stimulus generalization, (d) response generalization, (e) maintenance, (f) lifestyle change, and (g) social validity.

Positive Behavior

PBS intervention involves the use of strategies designed to make socially desirable responses (positive behaviors) more probable. Therefore, we examined whether positive behaviors did indeed increase following intervention. For each article we scored changes in positive behaviors from baseline to intervention. In illustration, consider a reinforcement-based procedure such as functional communication training. Because the procedure teaches specific communicative alternatives to problem behavior, one would expect to see increases in the level (i.e., frequency, percentage) of this alternative behavior following intervention. When data on communicative responses were reported in an article, we scored them. In principle, each reinforcement-based procedure should be associated with an increase in one or more types of positive behavior.

Likewise, stimulus-based procedures should promote positive behavior, by altering features of the environment. In illustration, consider a procedure such as interspersal training. When a difficult task demand (known to be discriminative for problem behavior) is interspersed among stimuli known to be discriminative for cooperation, one would expect an increase in the level of the latter positive

behavior. Again, in our synthesis we scored all data reflecting changes in positive behavior.

Problem Behavior

We measured another key outcome: whether an intervention produced a decrease in problem behavior. Intervention effects were always measured in terms of percentage reduction in problem behavior relative to baseline (using the calculation method described later in this review).

Stimulus Generalization

We measured stimulus generalization, defined as the degree to which intervention effects transferred from the original intervention situation to other situations involving new intervention agents, settings, and tasks. Stimulus generalization thus referred to a behavior change that occurred in spite of the fact that no planned intervention occurred in the new situation. We also measured the degree to which decreases in problem behavior generalized to new situations; this was also measured in terms of percentage reduction in problem behavior relative to baseline.

Response Generalization

We measured response generalization, defined as the degree to which intervention effects transferred from the initial target(s) of intervention to other aspects of the individual's behavior repertoire not targeted for intervention. Let's say an intervention targets ameliorating self-injurious behavior via communication training. The outcome may also demonstrate that aggressive behavior decreased and social play increased even though these two behaviors were not the focus of intervention. The desirable side effects of intervention (i.e., the decrease in aggression, and the increase in social play) constitute response generalization. Again, these effects were measured as percentage change from baseline.

Maintenance

Maintenance was defined as the degree to which intervention effects lasted over time (intervention durability). Maintenance was further defined as involving any of the following: (a) those data collected only after the specific intervention had been completely terminated; (b) data collected after the intervention had been modified (but not terminated) in some substantive way, such as a decrease in the number of formal intervention sessions per unit of time, a decrease in the number of intervention components in effect (i.e., intervention fading), or a gradual reduction in the involvement of the intervention agent (i.e., the agent decreases the amount of time given to intervention implementation). We measured maintenance effects as percentage reduction from baseline; when available, effects were noted at these specific follow-up periods: 1 to 5 months, 6 to 12 months, 13 to 24 months, and 25 months or more.

Lifestyle Change

Because the purpose of PBS is not simply to reduce the level of problem behavior, but also to enable individuals to live more normalized lives, a key outcome measure relates to lifestyle change. Positive lifestyle change was defined as increased engagement in normative social, vocational, family, recreational, and academic activities. Lifestyle change effects were measured, when available, as percentage increase from baseline.

Social Validity

Wolf (1978) argued that the impact of interventions cannot be gauged solely by objective measures. Unless significant others (e.g., parents, teachers, job coaches, friends, members of the community) perceive the intervention and its effects to be worthwhile, the intervention would be judged as inadequate. Considering this, social validity was also measured as an outcome.

We examined articles to determine whether rating scales were reported that tapped three critical dimensions of social validity: feasibility, desirability, and effectiveness. The generic feasibility dimension involved any variant of the question, "Would you be *able* to use this intervention strategy?" The generic desirability question involved any variant of the question, "Would you be *willing* to use this intervention strategy?" The effectiveness dimension was subdivided into (a) effectiveness with respect to reduction in problem behavior, and (b) effectiveness with respect to lifestyle change. Effectiveness with respect to problem behavior involved any variant of the question, "Does this intervention strategy reduce problem behavior to a level that is acceptable to you?" Effectiveness with respect to lifestyle change involved any variant of the question, "Does this intervention strategy make a difference in the lifestyle of the individual involved in terms of increasing opportunities to live, work, go to school, recreate, and socialize with typical peers and significant others in typical community settings?"

Summary

Using the terms just delineated, we scored those aspects of outcome measurement related to the following questions: (a) Were data available on positive behaviors resulting from the intervention (yes/no)? If so, specify the baseline and intervention data for each positive behavior. (b) Were data available on reduction in problem behavior following intervention (yes/no)? If so, specify the baseline and intervention data for each type of problem behavior reported. (c) Regarding stimulus generalization, were anecdotal observations available (yes/no)? Were direct observation data available (yes/no)? If direct observation data were available, specify the baseline and intervention data for problem behavior. (d) Regarding response generalization, were anecdotal observations available (yes/no)? Were direct observation data available (yes/no)? If direct observation data were available, specify the baseline and intervention data for socially appropriate behavior and problem behavior. (e) Regarding maintenance, were data on reduction in problem behavior noted at the following specified follow-up periods: 1 to 5 months, 6 to 12 months, 13 to 24 months, 25 months or more (yes/no for each)? If direct observation data were available, specify the baseline and intervention data. (f) Regarding lifestyle change, was a lifestyle change considered (anecdotally or formally) as a goal of the study (yes/no)? Was there a formal intervention to improve lifestyle (yes/no)? Was there measured success in producing a lifestyle change (yes/no)? If direct observation data were available on lifestyle change, specify the baseline and intervention data. (g) Regarding social validity, was there a generic feasibility question (yes/no)? Was there a generic desirability question (yes/no)? Was there a generic question regarding effectiveness with respect to reduction in problem behavior (yes/no)? Was there a generic question regarding effectiveness with respect to lifestyle change (yes/no)? For each of the preceding questions, specify the pre- and postintervention data for each scale.

Literature Search and Eligibility Criteria

We established initial selection criteria. Then we conducted a literature search using these criteria. Finally, we applied exclusion criteria to eliminate those articles that did not meet desired methodological standards.

Initial Selection Criteria

There were six criteria that guided the initial selection of articles from the literature. First, an article had to have been published between 1985 and 1996. All articles accessible to us by the cutoff date of December 31, 1996, were considered. Some 1996 journals had delayed publication dates in which the final issue for 1996 was released three to four months past the cutoff date. To compensate for the potential loss of relevant 1996 articles as well as to achieve the most up-to-date review, we included a small number (6) of *in press* articles that we had obtained prior to the cutoff date. These were classified as 1996 articles. (However, it should be noted that these 1996 articles were no longer *in press* by the time this review was completed and, therefore, are cited in the reference list as 1997 articles.)

Second, in an attempt to ensure high standards, only articles published in peer-reviewed journals were considered. Non-peer-reviewed manuscripts were not considered in the analysis in part to help ensure a uniformly high standard of experimental rigor, and in part because single-subject research tradition relies on the judgment of anonymous peer reviewers to confirm the presence of a functional relationship. The inclusion of non-peer-reviewed studies (e.g., dissertations, clinical trials) would have imposed uncontrolled sources of error, because each study would have required a surrogate peer review (by us) prior to inclusion to document the presence of experimental control.

Third, the article had to have been published in English.

Fourth, with respect to diagnosis, we examined all variations of DSM-III, DSM-III-R, DSM-IV, and AAMR classifications related to mental retardation, autism, and pervasive developmental disorder, either as a primary or secondary diagnosis. Thus, relevant dual diagnoses (e.g., anxiety disorder of childhood with mental retardation) were also retained.

Fifth, with respect to topography, the following types of problem behaviors were examined: self-injury, aggression, property destruction, and tantrums.

Sixth, with respect to intervention, all variations of stimulus- and reinforcement-based intervention, as defined earlier, were included.

Literature Search

We began by hand-searching all relevant education, psychology, and medical journals listed in four previous reviews that had included a consideration of PBS (Carr et al., 1990; Didden et al., 1997; Scotti et al., 1991; Scotti et al., 1996). The articles gleaned from this initial process produced references to additional research articles, review papers, books, book chapters, and newsletters. These

reference trails were, in turn, pursued. Additional reference trails were generated when the following abstract and index services were searched by crossing the disability diagnoses with the problem behavior topographies: *Child Development Abstracts and Bibliography, Current Contents/Social and Behavioral Sciences, ERIC, MEDLINE, Psychological Abstracts, PsychINFO, PsychLIT, PsychSCAN/MR,* and the *Social Science Citation Index.*

We also requested information on intervention for problem behavior from organizations having a stake in providing services for people with disabilities. The National Information Center for Children and Youth With Handicaps provided us with their list of 33 stakeholder organizations that included The Association for Persons With Severe Handicaps, The ARC (formerly the Association for Retarded Citizens), Autism Society of America, Council for Exceptional Children, and The National Down Syndrome Society.

Finally, we requested information from leading researchers (14), asking them to send us their published and *in press* papers dealing with the issue of problem behavior. We defined "leading researcher" as any individual having at least three published articles related to PBS.

Using the initial selection criteria and search methods just explicated, we identified 216 articles from 36 journals.

Exclusion Criteria

To ensure the highest quality database for subsequent analyses, we applied a number of methodological exclusion criteria to the initial sample of 216 articles. The application of these criteria resulted in a final sample of 109 articles that were included, and 107 that were excluded. (It should be

Table 1. Journals Examined and Number of Articles Included and Excluded

Journal	No. of articles included	No. of articles excluded
Adult Foster Care Journal	0	1
American Journal of Medical Genetics	1	0
American Journal on Mental Retardation (formerly American Journal of Mental Deficiency)	0	9
Analysis and Intervention in Developmental Disabilities	2	3
Applied Research in Mental Retardation	0	1
Augmentative and Alternative Communication	1	0
Australia and New Zealand Journal of Developmental Disabilities	1	3
Behavior Modification	6	5
Behavior Therapy	4	0
Behavioral Disorders	2	0
Behavioral Interventions	3	3
Behavioral Residential Treatment	3	13
Behaviour Research and Therapy	0	1
Behavioural Psychotherapy	0	5
Child and Family Behavior Therapy	1	1
Education and Training in Mental Retardation (formerly Education & Training of the Mentally Retarded)	3	7
Education and Treatment of Children	3	1
Exceptional Parent	0	1
Journal of Applied Behavior Analysis	46	14
Journal of the Association for Persons With Severe Handicaps	10	7
Journal of Autism and Developmental Disorders	2	5
Journal of Behavioral Education	2	0
Journal of Behavior Therapy and Experimental Psychiatry	4	2
Journal of Consulting and Clinical Psychology	1	0
Journal of Developmental and Physical Disabilities	4	5
Journal of Intellectual Disability Research	1	1
Journal of the Multihandicapped Person	2	0
Journal of Visual Impairment and Blindness	0	1
Mental Handicap Research	0	6
Mental Retardation	0	5
Research in Developmental Disabilities	3	2
School Psychology Review	3	0
Special Services in the Schools	1	0
Teaching Exceptional Children	0	1
The Irish Journal of Psychology	0	1
Topics in Early Childhood Special Education	0	3
Total	**109**	**107**

Note: The citation information for each included article appears in the Reference List, identified with an asterisk(*).

Table 2. Criteria Used to Exclude Articles From the Database

Exclusion criterion	Number of articles rejected
Absence of data	23
Inadequate design	28
Group design	12
Pooled data	33
Insufficient baseline data	31
Insufficient intervention data	7

Note: Some articles were rejected for more than one reason.

noted that some of the contributions made by the excluded studies will be discussed later in this publication.) Table 1 shows the breakdown of the two samples across the 36 journals.

Table 2 lists the six exclusion criteria used to select the final sample and the number of articles excluded for failing to meet a given criterion. Some articles were excluded for more than one reason, and thus the total is greater than 107.

There were 23 articles excluded because no data were reported (absence of data). These articles took the form of narrative case reports and extended anecdotes.

Twenty-eight articles were excluded because of inadequate design. Specifically, these articles involved empirical case reports that employed an AB design (i.e., a baseline (A) condition was followed by an intervention (B) condition). AB designs do not meet the internal validity criteria enunciated in standard methodology texts on single-subject research designs (e.g., Hersen & Barlow, 1976). In contrast, articles based on multiple baseline, reversal, and withdrawal designs, all meet these criteria (e.g., Hersen & Barlow, 1976), and were retained for analysis.

A small number of articles (12) used legitimate group designs involving a comparison between experimental and control groups. But these articles reported only group means, making it impossible to determine how any one individual responded to an intervention. Because all of our subsequent analyses depended on having individual data, the results of these articles could not be integrated into our final database. Further, 6 of these articles either failed to report critical data on problem behavior or pooled multiple measures in a way that made it impossible to retrieve data pertaining to problem behavior per se.

An additional 33 articles were excluded because they reported only pooled data; these articles did not use legitimate group designs but, rather, reported averaged pre/post measures for a group of participants with no control group. Again, the absence of data on any one individual precluded the possibility of integrating these data with the results obtained from other studies in which individual data were retrievable.

Thirty-one articles used acceptable single-subject designs but were nonetheless excluded because they reported fewer than three baseline points (often only 1

23

point). Our descriptive analyses (described later) required at least three baseline data points.

Likewise, seven articles were excluded because of insufficient intervention data (i.e., fewer than 3 intervention data points).

Data Collection Methods

How Intervention Effects Were Measured

One of the central issues we address is the impact of PBS on reducing problem behavior. We always measured intervention effects in terms of percentage reduction of problem behavior relative to baseline. Throughout the text, we will use the terms *percentage reduction* and *suppression measure* as synonyms. Many of the articles used a reversal design; that is, the intervention condition alternated several times with the baseline condition. When this type of design was used, we deemed the final, rather than earlier, intervention conditions most important, because the critical issue to be addressed concerned how well an individual was doing at the end of intervention. Additionally, because intervention frequently produced a steady downward trend in the level of problem behavior, the overall mean for an intervention condition could actually underrepresent the final effect. To minimize this difficulty, the mean of the last three intervention data points was used so that a judgment could be made concerning the degree of participant improvement at the termination of intervention. In sum, intervention effects were measured as the percentage reduction in problem behavior from the last three sessions of baseline compared

against the final three intervention sessions of the final intervention condition.

Frequently, a single participant received more than one type of intervention. For example, a participant might first be exposed to functional communication training, then choice, and finally interspersal training. That is, the person would have received one reinforcement-based intervention followed by two stimulus-based interventions, providing an opportunity to examine three outcomes. When this situation arose, we coded the data separately for each of the three outcomes. In contrast, if a participant had received choice in three different phases of a reversal design, we coded only the final outcome because, in this situation, the same stimulus-based intervention (choice) was simply repeated in each phase. So for a given participant, an outcome was defined as the data associated with each unique (nonrepetitive) variation of a reinforcement-based and/or stimulus-based intervention. Table 3 shows the number of outcomes per participant. As can be seen, out of a total of 230 participants, 145 (63%) produced a single outcome, while 85 (37%) produced more than one outcome. The total number of outcomes pooled across participants was 366.

To calculate percentage reduction in problem behavior (suppression measure), it was necessary to estimate the data from each article, point by point, thus generating the baseline and intervention data pertaining to the 366 outcomes. We measured, from the published tables and figures, the last three baseline points prior to intervention and, as noted previously, the last three intervention points of intervention. The intervention

Table 3. Relationship Between Outcomes and Participants

Number of participants	Number of outcomes per participant	Total number of outcomes
145	1	145
60	2	120
13	3	39
6	4	24
2	5	10
2	6	12
0	7	0
2	8	16

Note: The total number of participants was 230, and the total number of outcomes was 366.

mean was subtracted from the baseline mean, divided by the latter, and then multiplied by 100 to yield the percentage reduction from baseline. In illustration, consider a participant whose baseline frequency (last 3 data points) of aggressive behavior was 10, 12, and 14 aggressive acts, and whose intervention frequency (last 3 data points) of such behavior was 5, 1, and 0 acts. The baseline mean was thus 12, and the intervention mean 2. The percentage reduction from baseline was therefore (12 – 2) ÷ 12 x 100 = 83.3%. This method was used for data reported as a frequency or as a percentage of time samples observed. In a handful of cases (6), data were reported as latency to problem behavior (e.g., 10 s elapsed from the beginning of an observation session to the first instance of aggression; therefore, the latency to aggression was 10 s). In this case only, the data were transformed as follows. Any reported latency, irrespective of magnitude, was scored as 1 (i.e., problem behavior occurred after a specific time interval). The absence of problem behavior was scored as 0. Transforming the data set to this binary code permitted the calculations already described. In illustration, if the baseline were 1, 1, 1 and the intervention data were 1, 0, 0, then the percentage reduction would be 67%.

Recall that, in addition to evaluating the initial reduction in problem behavior following intervention, we also examined the data on positive behavior, stimulus generalization, response generalization, and maintenance. For these four outcome measures, intervention data were typically not reported; if they were, often fewer than three data points were available (e.g., a single data point on stimulus generalization might have been reported). To provide some indication of effectiveness regarding the four measures, we compared the three baseline data points with even one intervention point if that was all that was available. In illustration, if the baseline stimulus generalization data were 12, 14, and 16 self-injurious acts and the intervention stimulus generalization datum was 2 self-injurious acts, then the percentage reduction was (14 – 2) ÷ 14 x 100 = 85.7%.

How Reliability Was Measured

Three types of reliability were computed related to (a) adherence to initial selection and exclusion criteria; (b) agreement on scoring of categorical and continuous data; and (c) data entry (keystroke errors).

With respect to the initial selection and exclusion criteria, recall that the initial selection criteria produced 216 articles, and that the exclusion criteria resulted in 109 articles being retained, and 107 articles being excluded. We randomly chose 50 articles from the 109 that were retained, and 50 articles from the 107 that were excluded. We then gave these 100 articles to one of the coauthors who was not involved in the initial selection. This coauthor was asked to perform two rating tasks: (a) to apply the six initial selection criteria (described earlier) to the 100 articles and render a judgment as to whether the articles met these criteria, and (b) to apply the six exclusion criteria (described earlier) to the 100 articles and render a judgment as to whether the articles met these criteria. The rater agreed with the original coder's decision that all 100 articles met the initial selection criteria (100% reliability), and that the 50 articles that had been excluded by the original coder should indeed have been excluded as per the criteria used (100% reliability).

With respect to the categorical and continuous data, four coders scored these data from the 109 articles. Again, one of the coauthors not involved in the original scoring randomly selected 7 articles originally scored by each of the four coders and recoded all of the categorical and continuous data from this sample of 28 articles. Recall that the continuous data were based on the following variables: positive behavior, problem behavior, stimulus generalization, response generalization, maintenance, and lifestyle change. All the remaining variables (e.g., age, gender, problem behavior topography, etc.) were categorical. For the continuous data, the Pearson product-moment correlation, based on point-by-point reliability, was $+0.99$ ($p = .000$). For the categorical data, Kappa values (Cohen, 1960) ranged from .82 to 1.00. Landis & Koch (1977) characterized Kappa values greater than .75 as representing excellent agreement beyond chance.

With respect to data entry (keystroke errors), each of the four coders reentered data for seven randomly selected articles that they had previously scored. There was a total of 81,921 keystrokes across the four coders, of which 94 differed from the original entries, yielding an error rate of only 0.11%.

CHAPTER 3
RESULTS

As noted before, 109 published articles that met all the inclusion and exclusion criteria produced data on 230 participants involving 366 outcomes. We now present these data with respect to the research questions posed earlier in this review.

How Widely Applicable is PBS?

Table 4 displays the data on the characteristics of participants involved in PBS interventions as well as data on the type of intervention agent and type of intervention setting associated with the various participants. In a small number of cases, investigators failed to specify pertinent information (e.g., no diagnosis was given) or the description given was ambiguous (e.g., the participant was said to be "retarded" but no level of retardation was noted). Therefore, the numbers reported represent the percentage of the database for which each characteristic was adequately specified.

Approximately twice as many males as females were involved in PBS interventions. Although PBS was applied across the entire age range, preschool children were least likely to receive this type of intervention followed, in increasing order, by adolescents and adults (i.e., those 20 years of age and over); elementary-school-age children were most likely to receive intervention. The latter two age categories each accounted for one third of the participants.

About half the participants were diagnosed as having mental retardation, and one tenth as having autism. The remaining participants had combined diagnoses of retardation and/or autism, frequently accompanied by additional diagnoses (e.g., seizure disorder, brain damage). With respect to level of retardation, one third of the participants were functioning in the profound range, and another third in the severe range. The remaining participants were equally divided between the moderate and mild range.

The data on type of problem behavior showed that about one third of the participants displayed self-injurious behavior, and almost a quarter displayed aggression. Property destruction and tantrums were exhibited by only a small percentage of the participants. However, various combinations of the preceding four types of problem behavior were shown by fully one third of the participants.

PBS was a little more likely to be implemented by atypical intervention agents (e.g., psychologists, researchers) than typical agents (e.g., parents, teachers), although in a very small number of cases, both atypical and typical agents combined their efforts. In contrast, by a ratio of 2:1, interventions were more likely to occur in atypical settings (e.g., segregated schools, medical clinics) than typical settings (e.g., home, community, integrated schools).

In What Ways is the Field Evolving?

The field is evolving, as indicated by the ways in which selected aspects of the data set changed over time. These trends are presented next.

Table 4. Characteristics of Participants, Intervention Agents, and Settings

Characteristic	Number of cases	Percentage of database
Gender		
Male	150	67.6
Female	72	32.4
Age in years		
0-4	27	11.7
5-12	78	33.9
13-19	53	23.0
>20	72	31.3
Diagnosis		
Mental retardation (MR)	114	51.4
Autism (Aut)	25	11.3
MR + Aut	34	15.3
MR +/or Aut plus other diagnoses	49	22.1
Level of retardation		
Mild	32	16.7
Moderate	36	18.8
Severe	64	33.3
Profound	60	31.3
Type of problem behavior		
Aggression	51	22.2
Self-injurious behavior	78	33.9
Property destruction	6	2.6
Tantrums	11	4.8
Combinations	84	36.5
Intervention agent		
Typical	99	44.2
Atypical	120	53.6
Both typical and atypical	5	2.2
Intervention setting		
Typical	79	34.3
Atypical	150	65.2
Both typical and atypical	1	.4

Note: Number of cases does not always sum to 230 due to missing data.

Size of the Database

Figure 1 shows the data on the total number of articles, participants, and outcomes across 4-year blocks of time. In this and all subsequent figures, the numbers directly above each bar graph refer to the raw data, and the height of the bars refers to the data converted into percentages. In illustration, consider the data on articles published. Of the 109 articles, 24 (22%) were published between 1985 and 1988, 29 (26.6%) between 1989 and 1992, and 56 (51.4%) between 1993 and 1996. There is a substantial increase in the number of PBS articles published over time. It should be noted there were no patterns to the exclusion of articles across years. That is, our criteria did not result in more articles being excluded from early years than from recent years. Similar increases are seen for both the number of participants and the number of outcomes.

Demographics

Figure 2 shows the percentage of participants, by gender, in each 4-year block of time. In this and all subsequent figures (as was evident from Table 4), the data presented are for those cases on which information was available. Thus, although there were 230 participants in all, the gender for 8 of them was not identified (missing data), so percentages were computed for 222 participants rather than 230. Again, for this and subsequent figures, there was generally an increase in the number of participants over time, because greater numbers of articles were published over time. The important information, therefore, concerns the relative proportion of males to females over time. In each block of time, males were approximately twice as numerous as females.

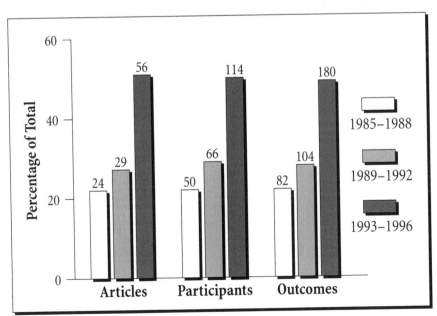

Figure 1. *Percentage of total articles (N = 109), participants (N = 230), and outcomes (N = 366) in each 4-year block of time. Numbers over each bar graph refer to the raw data (frequency counts).*

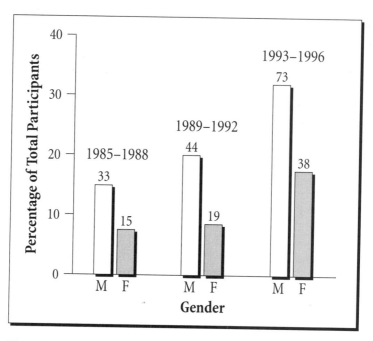

Figure 2. Percentage of total participants (N = 222) by gender in each 4-year block of time. Numbers over each bar graph refer to the raw data.

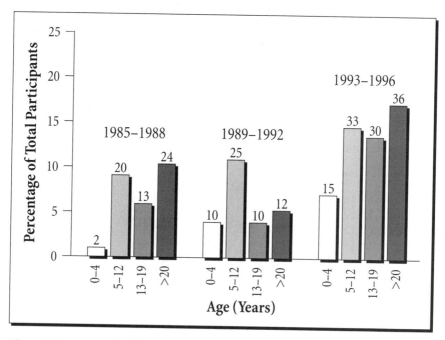

Figure 3. Percentage of total participants (N = 230) by age in each 4-year block of time. Numbers over each bar graph refer to the raw data.

Figure 3 shows the percentage of participants, by age, in each 4-year block of time. Generally, elementary-school-age children (5-12 years old), adolescents (13-19 years old), and adults (20 years and older) were well represented in each time block. Preschool children were generally less well represented.

Figure 5 shows the percentage of participants by level of mental retardation. Participants associated with profound and severe levels were generally more numerous in each block of time than those with moderate and mild levels of retardation.

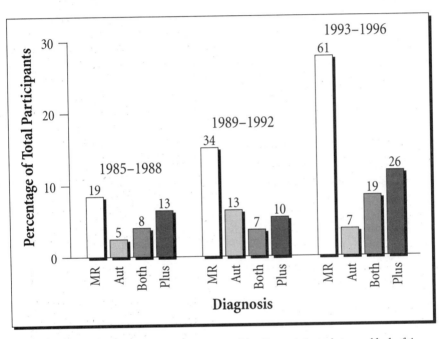

Figure 4. *Percentage of total participants (N = 222) by diagnosis in each 4-year block of time. Numbers over each bar graph refer to the raw data. MR = mental retardation; Aut = autism; Both = MR + Aut; Plus = MR &/or Aut plus other diagnoses.*

Figure 4 shows the percentage of participants, by diagnosis, over time. Participants with a diagnosis of mental retardation were most numerous in each time block with no clear trends evident for the other diagnoses.

Figure 6 shows the percentage of participants by types of problem behavior. In the first time block, aggression, self-injurious behavior, and combinations of problems were equally numerous. Over time, self-injurious behavior and combinations gradually became more numerous than aggression. Property destruction and tantrums remained at low levels across blocks of time.

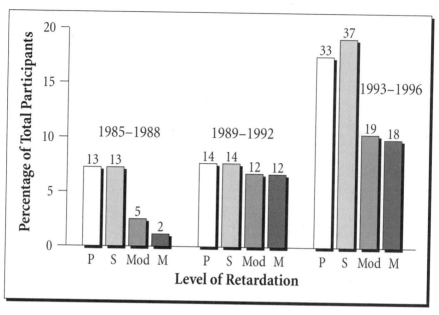

Figure 5. *Percentage of total participants (N = 192) by level of retardation in each 4-year block of time. Numbers over each bar graph refer to the raw data. P = profound; S = severe; Mod = moderate; M = mild.*

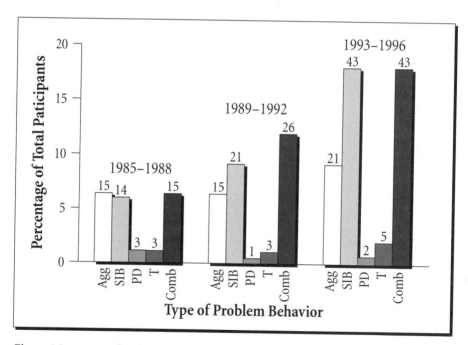

Figure 6. *Percentage of total participants (N = 230) by type of problem behavior in each 4-year block of time. Numbers over each bar graph refer to the raw data. Agg = aggression; SIB = self-injurious behavior; PD = property destruction; T = tantrums; Comb = combinations of types.*

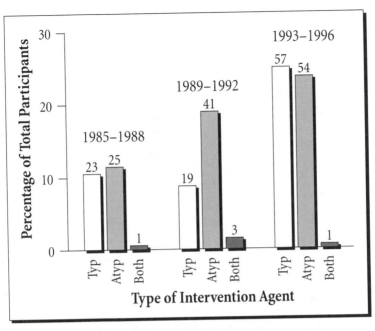

Figure 7. Percentage of total participants (N = 224) by type of intervention agent in each 4-year block of time. The numbers over each bar graph refer to the raw data. Typ = typical intervention agents; Atyp = atypical intervention agents; Both = both typical and atypical agents.

Figure 7 shows the percentage of participants involved with different types of intervention agents. Except for 1989-1992, typical and atypical agents were involved to the same degree. The involvement of both typical and atypical agents for the same participant was rare.

Figure 8 shows the percentage of participants by type of intervention setting. Although participants were most likely to be seen in atypical settings in each block of time, the gap between the use of atypical and typical settings steadily narrowed over time. The use of both atypical and typical settings for the same participant was rare.

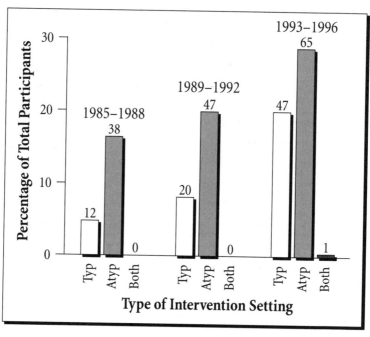

Figure 8. *Percentage of total participants (N = 230) by type of intervention setting in each 4-year block of time. The numbers over each bar graph refer to the raw data. Typ = typical intervention settings; Atyp = atypical intervention settings; Both = both typical and atypical settings.*

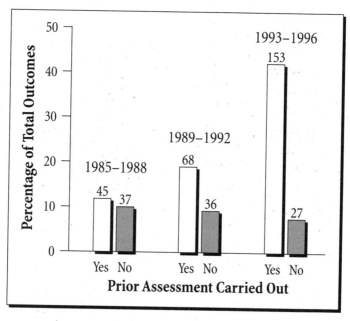

Figure 9. *Percentage of total outcomes (N = 366) by prior assessment in each 4-year block of time. The numbers over each bar graph refer to the raw data.*

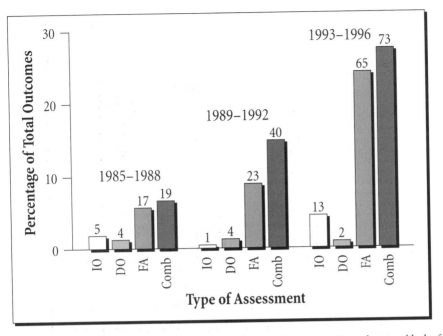

Figure 10. *Percentage of total outcomes (N = 266) by type of assessment in each 4-year block of time. Numbers over each bar graph refer to the raw data. IO = indirect observation; DO = direct observation; FA = functional analysis; Comb = combinations of 2 or more types of assessment.*

Assessment

Figure 9 shows the percentage of outcomes for which a prior assessment was (yes) or was not (no) carried out. There was a dramatic increase, over time, in the proportion of outcomes that were associated with a prior assessment compared to those that were not.

Figure 10 shows the percentage of outcomes for which a specific type of assessment was completed (i.e., indirect observation only, direct observation only, functional analysis only, and combinations of the preceding types of assessment). Over time, combined assessments and functional analysis became proportionately greater than indirect and direct observation.

Additional analyses permitted an answer to the question of whether assessment practices varied with respect to type of intervention agent, type of intervention setting, and whether intervention was subsequently carried out in all relevant contexts. With respect to type of intervention agent, for 257 outcomes it was possible to determine both the type of agent involved and the type of assessment involved. We contrasted the assessment data generated from formal functional analysis (FA-based) with the data based on less formal indirect and direct observation (not FA-based). FA-based procedures consisted of FA alone or FA used in combination with indirect or direct observation. Non-FA-based procedures excluded the use of FA and involved indirect and/or direct observation only. There were 200 outcomes that were FA-based. Of these, typical agents were associated with 73 outcomes (36.5% of the total), atypical agents with 124 outcomes (62.0% of the total), and both typical and atypical agents with 3 outcomes (1.5% of the total). There were 57 outcomes that were not FA-based. Of these, typical agents were associated with 41 outcomes (71.9% of the total), atypical agents with 14 outcomes (24.6% of the total), and both typical and atypical agents with 2 outcomes (3.5% of the total). In sum, FA-based outcomes were more likely to be associated with atypical agents, and non-FA-based outcomes were more likely to be associated with typical agents.

With respect to type of intervention setting, for 266 outcomes it was possible to determine both the type of setting involved and the type of assessment involved. There were 203 outcomes that were FA-based. Of these, typical settings were associated with 64 outcomes (31.5% of the total), and atypical settings with 139 outcomes (68.5% of the total). There were 63 outcomes that were not FA-based. Of these, 32 outcomes (50.8% of the total) were associated with typical settings, 30 outcomes (47.6% of the total), with atypical settings, and 1 outcome (1.6% of the total) with both typical and atypical settings. In sum, FA-based outcomes were more likely to be associated with atypical settings, and non-FA-based outcomes were equally likely in typical and atypical settings.

With respect to intervention in all relevant contexts, for 237 outcomes it was possible to determine whether intervention in all relevant contexts subsequently occurred, and the type of assessment preceding the intervention. There were 179 outcomes that were FA-based. Of these, 28 outcomes (15.6% of the total) were associated with intervention in all relevant contexts, but 151 outcomes (84.4% of the total) were not. Fifty-eight outcomes were not FA-based. Of these, 29 outcomes (50% of the total) were associated with intervention in all relevant contexts, and an equal number were not. In sum, FA-based outcomes were less likely to be associated with intervention in all relevant contexts, and non-FA-based were associated half the time with intervention in all relevant contexts and half the time without such intervention.

Overall, then, the use of functional analysis as an assessment tool is more closely associated with atypical agents, atypical settings, and a failure to intervene in all relevant contexts. In contrast, non-FA-based assessment is more closely associated with typical agents but is not differentially associated with type of setting or the presence versus absence of intervention in all relevant contexts.

Figure 11 shows the percentage of outcomes associated with each type of behavioral motivation for the 250 outcomes in which motivation (function) could be determined. In each block of time, escape predominated over other single motivations, and the degree to which this was the case increased over time. There was also some indication of a proportionate increase over time in the number of outcomes associated with multiple motivations (combinations of motivations).

Finally, there were only 11 outcomes (out of the total of 266) for which assessment was repeated over time. Between 1985 and 1988, 0 outcomes involved repeated assessments; between 1989 and 1993, there was 1 such outcome (.3% of the total); and between 1993 and 1996, there were 10 (3.8% of the total). Repeated assessment became more common over time, though the sample

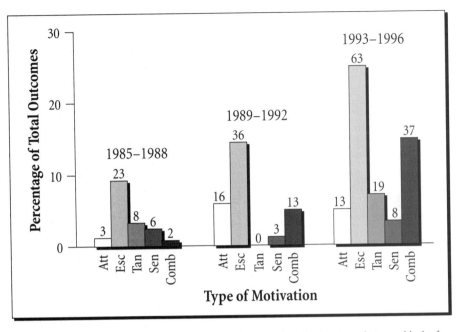

Figure 11. *Percentage of total outcomes (N = 250) by type of motivation in each 4-year block of time. Numbers over each bar graph refer to the raw data. Att = attention; Esc = escape; Tan = tangible; Sen = sensory; Comb = 2 or more types of motivation.*

size was very small. Our additional analyses allowed an answer to the question of when assessment was most/least likely to be repeated. Specifically, for 246 outcomes, it was possible to determine the type of setting and intervention agent for which the assessment was not repeated. With respect to settings, assessment was not repeated for 79 outcomes occurring in typical settings (32.1% of the total), 166 outcomes occurring in atypical settings (67.5% of the total), and 1 outcome occurring in both a typical and atypical setting (.4% of the total). With respect to intervention agents, assessment was not repeated for 106 outcomes occurring with typical agents (43.1% of the total), 136 outcomes occurring with atypical agents (55.3% of the total), and 4 outcomes occurring with both typical and atypical agents (1.6% of

the total). For 11 outcomes, it was possible to determine the type of setting and intervention agent for which the assessment was repeated. With respect to settings, assessment was repeated for 10 outcomes occurring in typical settings (90.9% of the total), 1 outcome occurring in atypical settings (9.1% of the total), and 0 outcomes occurring in both a typical and atypical setting. With respect to intervention agents, assessment was repeated for 8 outcomes occurring with typical agents (72.7% of the total), 2 outcomes occurring with atypical agents (18.2% of the total), and 1 outcome occurring with typical and atypical agents (9.1% of the total). In sum, then, assessment was most likely to be repeated with typical agents and settings, and most likely not to be repeated with atypical agents and settings.

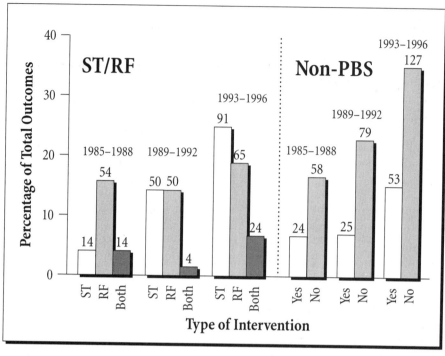

Figure 12. Percentage of total outcomes (N = 366) by type of intervention in each 4-year block of time. The numbers over each bar graph refer to the raw data. ST = stimulus-based intervention; RF = reinforcement-based intervention; Both = combined stimulus-based and reinforcement-based intervention; Non-PBS = nonpositive behavior support procedure was/was not (Yes/No) part of the intervention.

Intervention

Figure 12 shows the percentage of outcomes associated with various types of interventions. The relative proportion of stimulus-based versus reinforcement-based intervention reversed over time. Initially, reinforcement-based intervention predominated (1985-1988); then the two types of intervention were equally applied (1989-1992); and finally stimulus-based intervention predominated (1993-1996). Combined intervention (i.e., both stimulus-based and reinforcement-based) showed no clear trend relative to the other two types. Additional analyses permitted an answer to the question of when combined

intervention versus noncombined intervention (i.e., stimulus-based only or reinforcement-based only) was most/least likely to occur. Specifically, there were 42 outcomes for which combined intervention occurred. Of these, 26 (61.9% of the total) were carried out by typical agents and only 15 (35.7% of the total) were carried out by atypical agents. There were 324 outcomes for which noncombined intervention occurred. Of these, there were 9 outcomes for which type of agent could not be determined, leaving a database of 315 outcomes. For the remaining cases (315 outcomes), the pattern previously described was reversed. Specifically, only 128 (40.6% of the total) were carried out by typical agents, but 181 (57.5% of the total) were carried out by atypical agents. There were 7 outcomes involving both typical and atypical agents together (2.2% of the total).

Data were also available on type of setting. Of the 42 outcomes for which combined intervention occurred, 22 (52.4% of the total) were carried out in typical settings, and 19 (45.2% of the total) were carried out in atypical settings. In 1 outcome combined intervention was carried out in both typical and atypical settings (2.3% of the total). In sharp contrast, for the 324 outcomes involving noncombined intervention, 104 (32.1% of the total) were carried out in typical settings and 220 (67.9% of the total) were carried out in atypical settings. In sum, then, combined intervention was most likely to be conducted by typical agents and in typical settings, and noncombined intervention was most likely to be conducted by atypical agents and in atypical settings.

One final comparison concerns the relationship between type of intervention and its use in all relevant contexts. There were 322 outcomes for which it was possible to determine both the type of intervention used and whether it occurred in all relevant contexts. There were 285 outcomes associated with noncombined intervention. Of these, 50 (17.5% of the total) were associated with intervention in all relevant contexts, and 235 (82.5% of the total) were not. There were 37 outcomes associated with combined intervention. Of these, 26 (70.3% of the total) were associated with intervention in all relevant contexts, and 11 (29.7% of the total) were not. In sum, combined intervention was most likely to occur in all relevant contexts, whereas

noncombined intervention was least likely to occur in all relevant contexts.

Figure 12 also displays the data for outcomes associated with interventions that included a non-PBS component (yes) in addition to a PBS component versus outcomes not associated with interventions that included a non-PBS component (no) (i.e., the intervention had only PBS components). Consider the first block of time (1985-1988). There were 24 outcomes associated with interventions that included a non-PBS component, but 58 outcomes associated with interventions that did not include a non-PBS component. This pattern of results, namely, the predominance of outcomes for which PBS was the only component of the intervention package, was evident across each block of time.

Figure 13 shows the percentage of outcomes associated with different types of systems change. With respect to whether significant others were/were not (yes/no) required to change their behavior as a component of intervention, it is clear that the presence of such change predominated in all three time blocks; the degree of this predominance dramatically increased in the final time block. With respect to whether environmental reorganization was/was not (yes/no) a component of intervention, it is clear that the presence of such change was rare over time.

Figure 14 shows the percentage of outcomes in which intervention was/was not (yes/no) carried out in all relevant contexts. Over time, there was a dramatic increase in the number of outcomes associated with a failure to intervene in all relevant contexts, but only a modest increase in those associated with intervention in all relevant contexts. Additional analyses allowed us to

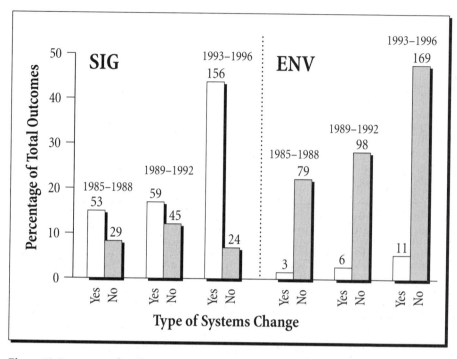

Figure 13. *Percentage of total outcomes (N = 366) by type of systems change in each 4-year block of time. The numbers over each bar graph refer to the raw data. SIG = significant others were required to change their behavior; ENV = environmental reorganization was undertaken.*

determine when intervention was most/ least likely to be carried out in all relevant contexts. Specifically, for 241 outcomes, it was possible to determine the type of setting and type of intervention agent for which intervention was not (no) carried out in all relevant contexts. With respect to settings, intervention was not carried out in all relevant contexts for 70 outcomes occurring in typical settings (29.0% of the total), and 171 outcomes occurring in atypical settings (71.0% of the total). With respect to agents, such intervention was not carried out for 82 outcomes occurring with typical agents (34.0% of the total), 157 outcomes occurring with atypical agents (65.1% of the total), and 2 outcomes occurring with both typical and atypical agents (1.0% of the total). For 72 outcomes, it was

possible to determine the type of setting and type of intervention agent for which intervention was (yes) carried out in all relevant contexts. With respect to settings, intervention was carried out in all relevant contexts for 42 outcomes occurring in typical settings (58.3% of the total), 29 outcomes occurring in atypical settings (40.3% of the total), and 1 outcome occurring in both typical and atypical settings (1.4% of the total). With respect to agents, such intervention was carried out for 62 outcomes occurring with typical agents (86.1% of the total), 5 outcomes occurring with atypical agents (6.9% of the total), and 5 outcomes occurring with both typical and atypical agents (6.9% of the total). In sum, then, intervention in all relevant contexts was most likely to occur with typical agents

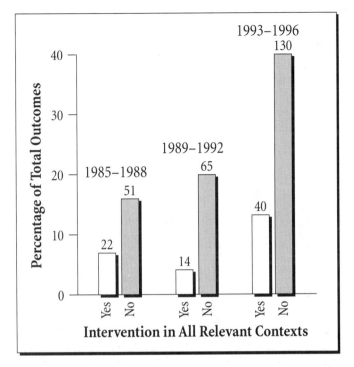

Figure 14. Percentage of total outcomes (N = 322) by intervention in all relevant contexts in each 4-year block of time. The numbers over each bar graph refer to the raw data. Yes = intervention was carried out in all relevant contexts; No = intervention was not carried out in all relevant contexts.

and settings, and most likely not to occur with atypical agents and settings.

Outcomes

Figure 15 shows the percentage of outcomes associated with diverse measures of generalization. Typically, data were based on small numbers of outcomes. The percentage of outcomes for stimulus generalization showed no trend over time, but that for response generalization showed a slight increase over time. The percentage of outcomes reported for maintenance for 1 to 5 months' duration rose steadily over time, but that for 6 to 12 months, and 13 to 24 months showed no trend. Likewise, no trends were seen for the percentage of outcomes associated

with a stated goal of lifestyle change, nor was there a trend with respect to the use of planned intervention intended to produce lifestyle change. Finally, the direct measurement of lifestyle change following intervention showed a small increase over time.

Figure 16 shows the percentage of outcomes associated with diverse measures of social validity. In all cases, data were based on very small numbers of outcomes. The percentage of outcomes for which there was a feasibility question showed a modest increase over time, but percentage for the desirability question showed no trend. Likewise, we noted a small increase for the question concerning the acceptability of the level of

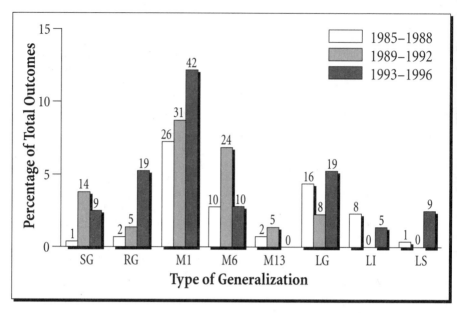

Figure 15. Percentage of total outcomes (N = 366) by type of generalization in each 4-year block of time. The numbers over each bar graph refer to the raw data. SG = stimulus generalization; RG = response generalization; M1, M6, and M13 = maintenance after 1–5 months, 6–12 months, and 13–24 months respectively; LG = stated goal of lifestyle change; LI = lifestyle change intervention implemented; LS = lifestyle change success measured.

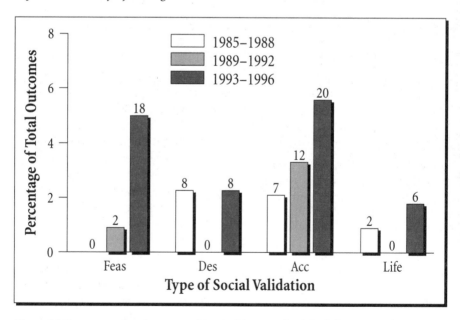

Figure 16. Percentage of total outcomes (N = 366) by type of social validation in each 4-year block of time. The numbers over each bar graph refer to the raw data. Feas = feasibility; Des = desirability; Acc = acceptability; Life = lifestyle change.

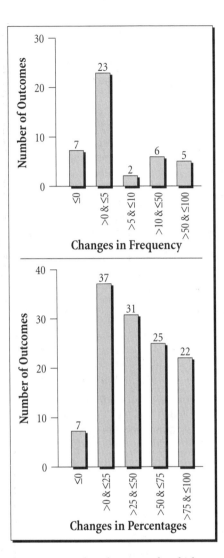

Figure 17. Number of outcomes for which changes in positive behavior were measured. The bar graph above represents the data for outcomes measured in terms of changes in frequency (N = 43), and the bar graph below represents the data for outcomes measured in terms of changes in percentages (N = 122). Numbers over each bar graph refer to the number of outcomes associated with each category of change.

problem-behavior reduction, but there was no trend concerning whether significant others perceived the intervention to have produced meaningful lifestyle change.

How Effective is PBS?

Changes in Positive Behavior

PBS intervention involves strategies designed to make socially desirable responses (positive behaviors) more probable. We identified data on changes in positive behavior for 165 of the 366 outcomes (45.1% of the total). Because the baseline for positive behavior was, in a substantial number of cases, 0, it was not possible to compute a percentage increase in positive behavior relative to baseline (because division by 0 is impermissible). Therefore, as Figure 17 shows, difference scores based on the raw data were used. For example, if the data were reported as frequencies (as they were in 43 cases), we simply subtracted the mean of the last three baseline points (typically 0) from the mean of the last three intervention points. In illustration, if the baseline mean was 0 communicative acts, and the intervention mean was 30 communicative acts, then the difference score (i.e., increase in communicative acts) was 30. In Figure 17, this data outcome would contribute to the bar graph category >10 & ≤50. We used the same formula for data reported as percentages (as they were in 122 cases). In illustration, if the baseline mean was 10% intervals of cooperative behavior, and the intervention mean was 90% intervals of cooperative behavior, then the difference score (i.e., increase in percentage of intervals containing cooperative behavior) was 80%. Figure 17 displays both the frequency and percentage data on positive behavior. In either category, frequency or percentages, interval data are not directly comparable. For example, a frequency increase of 50 communicative acts is not "twice as good" as a frequency increase of 25 cooperative acts. The two types of behavior are not equivalent. Nonetheless, the data in Figure 17 are presented to provide information to answer the general question of whether positive behaviors did indeed increase following PBS. The figure shows clearly that there were only a handful of cases in which the level of positive behavior remained the same or decreased following intervention. Overwhelmingly, for both the frequency and percentage data, positive behaviors increased following the use of PBS, albeit the degree of increase varied widely from modest to substantial.

Distribution of Outcome Effectiveness for PBS Interventions

Table 5 shows the distribution of outcome effectiveness in terms of percentage

reduction in problem behavior from baseline. Across all PBS interventions (i.e., irrespective of whether they were stimulus-based or reinforcement-based), approximately two-thirds of the outcomes (68.0%) were associated with substantial reductions in problem behavior of 80% or more from baseline levels. A similar pattern was seen when the total database for intervention was subdivided: outcomes that were stimulus-based versus those that were reinforcement-based. Specifically, 66.5% of the outcomes that were stimulus-based and 71.6% of the outcomes that were reinforcement-based demonstrated 80% or more reduction in problem behavior from baseline levels. In contrast, across the intervention categories, a minimal number of outcomes were associated with small reductions (i.e., less than 20% reduction from baseline levels). For approximately 6 to 8% of the outcomes, depending on the type of intervention, an increase in problem behavior was noted. It would be interesting to know whether there are specific variables that predict the few instances in which PBS produced minimal or negative

Table 5. Distribution of Outcome Effectiveness: Reduction in Problem Behavior

	Frequency of outcomes by percentage reduction in problem behavior								
	100%	90-99%	80-89%	60-79%	40-59%	20-39%	0-19%	Increase in problem behavior	Total outcomes
All PBS-based outcomes	97	92	60	51	23	10	6	27	366
ST-based outcomes	44	52	35	31	12	6	5	12	197
RF-based outcomes	67	48	36	25	12	4	2	17	211

Note: PBS = any intervention that had an ST and/or RF component; ST = any stimulus-based intervention (i.e., ST with/without RF, with/without non-PBS); RF = any reinforcement-based intervention (i.e., RF with/without ST, with/without non-PBS). Thus, outcomes associated with ST and RF in combination would appear once under ST-based and again under RF-based.

effects. But the articles reviewed provided insufficient information to make such a determination. A reasonable working hypothesis is that intervention failures are more a function of systems than of techniques. Thus, uncooperative staff, too many staff changes, lack of respite for parents, and insufficient time on the part of teachers are all plausible examples of the types of systemic factors likely to impact negatively on intervention outcomes, a point taken up again later. At present, the existence of unfavorable outcomes should serve as a prompt for researchers to expand their search for those systems variables that appear to influence outcome.

Success Rates for PBS Interventions Pooled Across Outcomes

Table 6 shows the success rates for various types of PBS interventions. A stringent criterion was used to define success: An outcome had to reflect a 90% or greater reduction in problem behavior from baseline levels to be considered a success. The success rate was generally within 5 points of 50%, irrespective of the type of intervention employed.

Almost three-quarters of the interventions (72.1%) did not include a non-PBS component; however, the presence versus absence of a non-PBS

Table 6. Success Rates for PBS Interventions Pooled Across Outcomes

Pooled data	Number of outcomes	Percentage of grand total	Number of successes	Percentage of of successes
All interventions (grand total)	366	100	189	51.6
All that excluded non-PBS	264	72.1	136	51.5
All that included non-PBS	102	27.9	53	52.0
All single interventions	324	88.5	167	51.5
All ST interventions	155	42.3	74	47.7
All ST excl. non-PBS	129	35.2	59	45.7
All ST incl. non-PBS	26	7.1	15	57.7
All RF interventions	169	46.2	93	55.0
All RF excl. non-PBS	104	28.4	62	59.6
All RF incl. non-PBS	65	17.8	31	47.7
All combined interventions	42	11.5	22	52.4
All ST + RF that excl. non-PBS	31	8.5	15	48.4
All ST + RF that incl. non-PBS	11	3.0	7	63.6

Note: ST = stimulus-based interventions; RF = reinforcement-based interventions; excl. = excluding; incl. = including. Success was defined as a 90% or more reduction in problem behavior from baseline.

Table 7. Types of Non-PBS Interventions Used

Type of non-PBS	Number of outcomes
Extinction	58
DRO	6
Punishment	49
Reprimand	4
Forced compliance	6
Response cost	8
Overcorrection	6
Timeout	7
Brief restraint	17
Water mist	1

Note: The total number of outcomes added up to more than 102, because some outcomes were associated with several types of non-PBS.

component had little effect on intervention success (i.e., each intervention type produced success rates close to 50%). A substantial majority of interventions (88.5%) used stimulus-based strategies or reinforcement-based strategies, but not both together. The two strategies were used about equally often. The success rates for the two were comparable (i.e., 47.7% for stimulus-based, and 55.0% for reinforcement-based). Only a small minority of interventions (11.5%) combined stimulus-based with reinforcement-based strategies. These combined interventions also produced success rates of about 50%. The one exception to this general finding involved combined interventions that included one or more non-PBS interventions; these produced a 63.6% success rate. However, this rate was based on the smallest number of outcomes for any of the PBS intervention categories reported and may, therefore, reflect sampling error rather than a unique property of this type of intervention.

Because non-PBS interventions were associated with approximately one quarter (102) of the 366 outcomes, it is helpful to clarify the specific nature of these interventions. Table 7 presents a breakdown of the types of non-PBS interventions used. About half the outcomes were associated with the use of extinction and half with the use of punishment. A handful were associated with DRO. The punishment category was further broken down into seven procedures. Of these, only brief physical restraint was associated with more than eight outcomes. Among the seven punishment procedures, only water mist has been considered in the literature (Scotti et al., 1991) as a highly intrusive procedure, and it was associated with only 1 outcome of the 102 generated.

Table 8. Generalization Measures of Outcome Effectiveness

	Frequency of outcomes by percentage reduction in problem behavior								
								Increase in	
	100%	90-99%	80-89%	60-79%	40-59%	20-39%	0-19%	problem behavior	Total outcomes
Stimulus generalization outcomes	5	8	3	2	1	0	0	1	20

	Frequency of outcomes by percentage increase in appropriate behavior								
								Decrease in	
	100%	90-99%	80-89%	60-79%	40-59%	20-39%	0-19%	appropriate behavior	Total outcomes
Response generalization outcomes	0	1	2	3	4	1	1	1	13

Stimulus and Response Generalization

Stimulus generalization refers to the degree to which intervention effects transferred from the original intervention situation to other situations involving new intervention agents, settings, and tasks. Anecdotal reports of stimulus generalization were noted for 29 outcomes. Data-based reports of stimulus generalization were noted for an additional 24 outcomes (i.e., in 6.6% of the total database). However, in 4 of these cases, the baseline data were inadequate for computation purposes (i.e., fewer than 3 data points were reported). The distribution of the remaining 20 outcomes is shown in Table 8 (top half). As can be seen, in a number of cases, problem behavior decreased from baseline levels, sometimes substantially, in situations that were not a direct target of intervention.

Response generalization refers to the degree to which intervention effects transferred from the initial behavioral target of intervention to other aspects of an individual's behavior repertoire that were not targeted for intervention. In the articles examined, response generalization consisted exclusively of changes in a variety of appropriate behaviors (e.g., social skills, academics). Anecdotal reports of response generalization were noted for 25 outcomes. Data-based reports of response generalization were noted for an additional 26 outcomes (i.e., in 7.1% of the total database). However, in 13 of these cases, baseline data were inadequate (i.e., fewer than 3 data points were reported), or baseline data were reported but postintervention data were not. The distribution of the remaining 13 outcomes is shown in Table 8 (bottom half). As can be seen, in a number of cases, modest increases in appropriate behavior were observed relative to baseline, even though such behavior was not a target of intervention.

Table 9. Maintenance Measures of Outcome Effectiveness

| | Frequency of outcomes by percentage reduction in problem behavior | | | | | | | |
	100%	90-99%	80-89%	60-79%	40-59%	20-39%	0-19%	Increase in problem behavior	Total outcomes
1 - 5 months	62	6	8	14	1	2	1	5	99
6 - 12 months	19	9	5	5	4	2	0	0	44
13 - 24 months	5	0	1	0	1	0	0	0	7

Note: There were no maintenance outcomes reported for follow-up periods of 25 months or more.

Maintenance

As noted earlier, maintenance is defined as the degree to which intervention effects were documented to last over time (intervention durability). Table 9 displays the outcome data for maintenance, measured as percentage reduction in problem behavior from baseline, noted at specific follow-up periods, namely, at 1 to 5 months, 6 to 12 months, 13 to 24 months, and 25 months or more. The number of outcomes noted for each of the follow-up periods just mentioned was 99, 44, 7, and 0, indicating a dramatic decrease in available data with each successive increase in maintenance duration. In general, most outcomes clustered at the high end of the percentage reduction in problem behavior. That is, good maintenance effects were observed for a substantial majority of outcomes. Using a success criterion of 90% or more reduction in problem behavior from baseline, the success rates at 1 to 5 months, 6 to 12 months, and 13 to 24 months were 68.7%, 63.6%, and 71.4% respectively, suggesting that intervention effects were quite durable, at least for those cases in which maintenance outcome data were available.

Lifestyle Change

As the ultimate purpose of PBS is to enable individuals to live more normalized lives, lifestyle change is an important index of effectiveness. Surprisingly, the database for this outcome measure was extremely small. Lifestyle change was a stated intervention goal for only 24 out of the 230 participants in the sample (i.e., 10.4% of the sample). A formal intervention directed specifically at improving lifestyle was recorded for 8 out of the 230 participants (i.e., 3.5% of the sample). Finally, success in improving lifestyle was measured for only 6 participants (i.e., 2.6% of the sample). Of these, anecdotal (nonquantified) improvement was noted for 4 participants. Data (percentage improvement from baseline) were taken on only 2 participants, and showed a 100% improvement with respect to increased engagement in community activities.

Social Validity

Social validity refers to whether significant others (e.g., parents, teachers, job coaches) perceive the intervention and its effects to be worthwhile. (It should be noted that no study involved asking persons with disabilities what they thought about the social validity of the interventions that they experienced.) Again, various aspects of social validity were assessed for a very small number of participants. With respect to the generic feasibility question (e.g., "Would you be able to use this intervention strategy?"), data were available on 14 of the 230 participants. In 8 cases, these data were anecdotal; teachers (for example) stated that they had continued to use the intervention over time. For the remaining 6 participants, Likert-scale data indicated that whereas intervention agents thought they would seldom/never be able to use the intervention before they had been trained, afterwards they felt they would very much/always be able to use the intervention.

In terms of the generic desirability question (e.g., "Would you be willing to use this intervention strategy?"), data were available on 12 participants. In 7 cases, these data were anecdotal statements from support people affirming the desirability of the intervention used over all other proposed or previously attempted interventions. For the remaining 5 participants, Likert-scale data were available. These data showed that, prior to training, support people felt they would choose to implement the intervention never/not at all; following training, they would choose the intervention very much/always.

With respect to the generic acceptability question (e.g., "Does the intervention strategy reduce problem behavior to a level that is acceptable to you?"), data were available for 29 participants. In 4 cases, these data were anecdotal. Support people were interviewed and asserted that each of the participants had "improved." In 25 cases, data were available

but the metric used varied greatly from study to study. For example, in 6 cases, support people were asked to rate the degree to which (strongly agree/agree/ uncertain/disagree/strongly disagree) they felt that the participant's problem behavior had improved. In 4 of these cases, 65% of the support people strongly agreed/agreed; in the other 2 cases, 83% strongly agreed/agreed. In 2 cases, support people were asked to rate problem behavior on a 6-point scale (where 1 represented low improvement and 6, high improvement). In 1 case, the rating improved from 1.8 to 2.9; in the other case, from 2.2 to 4.1. In 13 additional cases, significant others were asked to rate problem behavior on a 7-point scale (where 1 represented low improvement and 7, high improvement). For 8 of these cases, the ratings improved from a preintervention mean of 2.1 to a post-intervention mean of 5.1. For 5 of these cases, the postintervention mean was 5.9, but no preintervention data were reported, complicating interpretation. Finally, in 4 cases, significant others were asked to use a 10-point scale (where 1 was little/no improvement and 10 was maximum improvement/no problem behavior). The preintervention mean was 2.1, and the postintervention mean was 7.2.

For the generic lifestyle change question (e.g., "Does this intervention strategy produce effects that increase opportunities to live, work, go to school, recreate, and socialize with typical peers and significant others in typical community settings?"), data were available for 8 participants. In 6 of these cases, lifestyle change was rated on a 7-point scale (where 1 represented little improvement and 7, major improvement). Across 3 of these cases, the preintervention mean was 2.3, and the postintervention mean, 6.0.

In the other 3 cases, the postintervention mean was 3.2, but there were no preintervention data, again complicating interpretation. In the remaining 2 cases, significant others were interviewed by phone 2 years after intervention and asked whether they agreed/disagreed that family interactions had improved as a consequence of intervention and that the child was more accepted in the community; 86% of the interviewees agreed with the preceding statement.

What Factors Modulate the Effectiveness of PBS?

The data on intervention effectiveness, just examined, make clear that stimulus-based and reinforcement-based interventions produced very similar outcomes. Of course it is possible that each type of intervention might, nonetheless, produce a unique interaction with modulator variables such as demographic characteristics or type of assessment used. However, from a clinical perspective, there are no *pure* interventions. That is, clinically, stimulus-based intervention always encompasses changes in reinforcement parameters (e.g., redesigning a curriculum will also produce shifts in the allocation of reinforcers across behaviors), and reinforcement-based intervention always encompasses changes in stimulus parameters (e.g., a reinforcer is, itself, a stimulus that can be discriminative for specific responses). These facts led to our decision to pool all the data for the two types of intervention in order to study how various factors modulate the effectiveness of PBS-based intervention as a whole. Because clinical practice always involves combining elements of stimulus- and reinforcement-based

intervention, we assume that pooling the data across the two types of intervention provides one plausible estimate of the outcomes of comprehensive positive behavior support applied to an individual.

Influence of Demographic Variables

Table 10 displays the relationship between different demographic variables and intervention effectiveness across all PBS-based outcomes. The first entry, for gender, shows that the percentage of success was not strongly influenced by gender per se; both males and females showed equivalent success rates (i.e., within a few points of 50%).

The data on age show considerable variation, from a success rate of 41.1% for adults (i.e., participants over 20 years of age) to a success rate of 63.7% for adolescents, with preschool and school-age children falling between these two extremes. The relationship between age and success rate appears linear up to adolescence, and drops off sharply thereafter.

With respect to diagnosis, the success rate was highest for those diagnosed with a combination of mental retardation plus autism (59.1%), and lowest for those diagnosed with autism alone (43.2%). The other two diagnostic categories were associated with success rates that fell between those just given. It is interesting to note that the diagnostic categories associated with the smallest number of outcomes (autism, and mental retardation plus autism) were also the two whose success rates deviated most sharply from the typical finding (in this synthesis) of a 50% success rate, suggesting the influence of sampling error rather than formal diagnosis per se.

Table 10. Relationship Between Demographic Variables and Outcome Effectiveness

Characteristic	Number of outcomes	Number of successes	Percentage of successes
Gender			
Male	235	128	54.5
Female	117	60	51.3
Age in years			
0-4	37	17	45.9
5-12	129	70	54.3
13-19	88	56	63.7
>20	112	46	41.1
Diagnosis			
Mental retardation (MR)	201	106	52.7
Autism (Aut)	37	16	43.2
MR + Aut	44	26	59.1
MR +/or Aut plus other diagnoses	72	35	48.6
Level of retardation			
Mild	51	23	45.1
Moderate	53	35	66.0
Severe	100	53	53.0
Profound	110	58	52.7
Type of problem behavior			
Aggression	90	50	55.5
Self-injurious behavior	132	74	56.1
Property destruction	13	5	38.5
Tantrums	13	8	61.6
Single type	248	137	55.2
Combination of types	118	52	44.1

Note: Number of outcomes does not always sum to 366 due to missing data.

Level of retardation produced a pattern of results similar to those just noted for diagnosis. Specifically, the two retardation levels associated with the greatest number of outcomes (severe and profound) had success rates within a few points of 50%. Those associated with the fewest number of outcomes (mild and moderate) had success rates that deviated from the 50% rate (i.e., 45.1% and 66.0% respectively), again suggesting the influence of sampling error rather than level of retardation per se.

Table 11. Relationship Between Assessment Variables and Outcome Effectiveness

Factor	Number of outcomes	Number of successes	Percentage of successes
Type of assessment			
Informal observation	19	8	42.1
Formal direct observation	10	6	60.0
Functional analysis	105	64	61.0
Combined assessments	132	79	59.8
Assessment conducted	266	157	59.0
No assessment conducted	100	32	32.0
Type of function			
Attention	32	20	62.5
Escape	122	75	61.5
Tangible	27	15	55.6
Sensory	17	4	23.5
Multiple	52	33	63.5
Assessment repeated			
Yes	11	4	36.4
No	255	155	60.0
Assessment information used			
Yes	231	135	58.4
No	35	22	62.9

Type of problem behavior produced success rates near 50% for those behaviors associated with numerous outcomes (i.e., aggression and self-injurious behavior), and considerable deviations from 50% for those behaviors associated with few outcomes (i.e., property destruction and tantrums). Importantly, it was possible to cumulate all outcomes involving a single type of problem behavior (e.g., aggression alone, self-injurious behavior alone, etc.) and compare these to all outcomes involving combinations of problem behavior (e.g., aggression plus self-injurious behavior, property destruction plus aggression, etc.). The success rate for outcomes based on single types was 55.2%, whereas the rate for combinations was only 44.1%. Because this comparison involved large numbers of outcomes, the approximately 11% spread between the two success rates suggests that successfully intervening on combinations of problem behavior may be somewhat more difficult than intervening on single types of problem behavior.

Influence of Assessment Variables

Table 11 displays the relationship between different assessment variables and intervention effectiveness. The data suggest that conducting an assessment can have a considerable impact on success rates. Thus, conducting some kind of assessment (i.e., informal observation, formal direct observation, functional analysis, or any combination of these three) was associated with a success rate of 59.0%, whereas a failure to conduct assessment was associated with a success rate of 32.0%. Functional analysis and combined assessment each yielded success rates close to 60%, as did formal direct observation. Informal observation produced the lowest success rate (42.1%); however, both informal observation and formal direct observation were based on very small numbers of cases, and these results may reflect sampling error.

The success rates associated with type of function were always within a few points of 60% irrespective of whether the function was attention, escape, tangible, or multiple types (i.e., the problem behavior was maintained by more than one factor). The one exception to this finding involves the sensory function, which produced a dramatically lower success rate (23.5%). The latter success rate may reflect the fact that sensory functions are nonsocial in nature, whereas all the other functions are socially mediated. Alternatively, the difference may merely reflect sampling error given the fact that the data on sensory function were based on a very small number of outcomes.

Table 11 also addresses the issue of whether repeating functional assessment over time influences success rates. The data showed that repeated assessments were associated with lower success rates (36.4%) than single assessments (60.0%). However, the former rate is difficult to interpret because it is based on only 11 outcomes, again plausibly reflecting sampling error. Alternatively, this finding may reflect the fact that repeated assessments were more likely if the initial intervention proved unsuccessful or if the factors controlling the behavior were more complex.

Finally, the data show that success rates were equivalent and high whether or not the assessment data were used to design an intervention. However, the failure to use the assessment data was a characteristic of only 35 outcomes. In addition, it was not possible to determine from the published reports whether mere knowledge of assessment data nonetheless influenced choice of intervention in subtle ways not articulated by the investigator.

Systems Change

Table 12 shows that the two systems-change variables may have had an effect on success rates. Thus, when significant others (e.g., teachers, parents, job coaches) altered their own behavior as part of a systematic intervention, the success rate was 55.2%, which was higher than the 41.8% success rate associated with interventions that did not involve behavior change on the part of significant others. Likewise, environmental reorganization was associated with a success rate of 65.0%, higher than the rate obtained without such organization (50.9%). However, the latter finding must be interpreted cautiously, because there were so few outcomes associated with environmental reorganization.

Table 12. Relationship Between Systems-Change Variables and Outcome Effectiveness

Factor	Number of outcomes	Number of successes	Percentage of successes
Significant others change			
Yes	268	148	55.2
No	98	41	41.8
Environmental reorganization			
Yes	20	13	65.0
No	346	176	50.9

Table 13. Relationship Between Ecological Validity and Outcome Effectiveness

Factor	Number of outcomes	Number of successes	Percentage of successes
Intervention agent			
Typical	154	94	61.0
Atypical	196	87	44.3
Intervention setting			
Typical	126	61	48.4
Atypical	239	128	53.5
Intervene in all relevant contexts			
Yes	76	42	55.3
No	246	127	51.6

Note: Data based on combinations of both typical and atypical intervention agents and settings were omitted, because there were too few outcomes.

Ecological Validity

With respect to ecological validity, the data (Table 13) show that the type of intervention agent may make a difference. Typical agents (e.g., parents, teachers) produced a success rate of 61.0%, whereas atypical agents (e.g., psychologists, researchers) had a success rate of only 44.3%. With respect to type of setting, the success rates for typical (e.g., home, integrated school) versus atypical (e.g., clinic, institution) were roughly comparable. Comparability in success rates was also seen for interventions that took place in all relevant contexts versus those that did not.

Medication

In light of the well-developed pharmacotherapy literature alluded to earlier (Reiss

& Aman, 1998; Schaal & Hackenberg, 1994; Schroeder & Tessel, 1994; Thompson et al., 1991), it seems plausible that medication might be another variable that modulates the effectiveness of PBS. However, in many of the studies examined, no reference was made to medication, so its use is an unknown. In still other studies, reference was made to medication, but the dosage level was not indicated nor was the duration of drug use specified. A minority of studies provided details on dosage level and duration but did not report data on how medication and PBS interrelated. Thus, the unique contributions made by medication versus PBS are not known at this time. More important, perhaps, the possibility that combinations of PBS and medication produce synergistic effects has not been examined systematically and is clearly a topic that merits future attention from researchers.

CHAPTER 4
DISCUSSION

The results of our synthesis bear on several important issues: (a) potential biases in the retrieved literature, (b) inferences based on the results, (c) effectiveness of PBS, and (d) implications for future research.

Potential Biases in the Retrieved Literature

Rigor Versus Relevance?

Our exclusion criteria (Table 2) were designed to produce a database that met the highest standards of methodological rigor currently articulated in the field. These standards, however, reflect a strong bias in favor of demonstrations of experimental control (internal validity), sometimes at the expense of demonstrations of generality (external validity). These standards emphasize the analysis of cause and effect relationships at the level of single individuals with a view to understanding process variables. This does not mean, however, that the single-subject designs that predominate in the field are inherently unable to address the issue of external validity.

It will be helpful to review, briefly, the difference between group methods and single-subject designs with respect to the issue just raised. Traditional group methods rely on sampling procedures to establish external validity. Greater generality is possible for individuals who are similar to research participants on relevant characteristics, and generally external validity is less reliable for individuals who are different from research participants on those character-

istics. In the case of single-subject designs, the investigator's ability to generalize to other individuals is dependent on an understanding of what factors controlled a participant's behavior in baseline (Wolery & Ezell, 1993). Once an investigator understands what controls baseline responding, then applying interventions to other participants whose behavior is controlled by variables similar to those identified in the baseline will likely produce greater external validity than that achievable in the absence of such similarity.

Single-subject research, now almost four decades old, has been invaluable in identifying critical variables that control problem behavior, raising issues concerning assessment and intervention, and suggesting broad guidelines for remediation. It is also true, however, that this style of rigorous experimental research is easiest to carry out in controlled situations. This contributed to the large number of outcomes in our database that involved atypical intervention agents (especially researchers and other expert professionals), atypical settings (particularly noncommunity settings in which key variables could be easily monitored and manipulated), and restricted venues for intervention (i.e., a lack of intervention in all relevant contexts). Short-term process studies conducted in restricted contexts also tend to underemphasize repeated assessment, multicomponent intervention, and measures of generalization, maintenance, and validated lifestyle change. Yet, as we noted earlier, these are precisely the dimensions that define relevance (external validity), because without them there is no demonstration that an intervention (a) is readily applicable in the community or (b) changes peoples' lives in broad, meaningful ways. In view of what we have just outlined, it is not surprising that the journal best known for its emphasis on experimental analysis (*Journal of Applied Behavior Analysis*) accounted for almost half (42%) of the articles included in the database (Table 1) whereas the journal best known for its applied community orientation (*Journal of The Association for Persons With Severe Handicaps*) accounted for only 9% of the articles included.

Have researchers chosen rigor over relevance? It seems so. Is this choice the only one possible for the field? We think not.

Rigor Over Relevance?

With respect to the issue of rigor over relevance, there is much research, including some in our database, that does in fact demonstrate a systematic concern for external validity and all the variables associated with it. In addition, many of the excluded articles, while not meeting our methodological criteria, easily met important criteria for external validity, and for that reason will be highlighted shortly. Finally, our review of the research literature should not be seen as an exact reflection of current clinical practice. There is a vast nonresearch (practitioner) literature that reports successful, externally valid applications of PBS (e.g., Copeland, 1997; Hays, 1997; Jones, 1997; Kincaid, 1992, 1996; Lucyshyn & Albin, 1993; Metlen, Majure, & Stroll-Reisler, 1996; Metz, 1992a, 1992b, 1992c; The Family Connection staff, DeVault, Krug, & Fake, 1996; Tifft, 1996; Turnbull & Turnbull, 1996; Virginia Institute for

Developmental Disabilities, 1996). The challenge therefore is how best to view the bias toward controlled experimental research so that new perspectives can be created that build constructively on that bias while at the same time moving beyond it.

The bias toward controlled experimental research is a legitimate beginning for the evaluation of the PBS approach. Recall that two questions critical to this synthesis (and discussed shortly) involve (a) whether PBS is effective and (b) what factors modulate its effectiveness. These questions can be definitively answered only through careful experimental analysis that includes appropriate controls to ensure internal validity. In the absence of these controls, interpretation of the database would be speculative at best. Nonetheless, the portions of the database that emphasize internal validity while minimizing the focus on external validity are a useful beginning for the field, because they increase our confidence that (a) PBS procedures do have demonstrable effectiveness and (b) certain variables are causal in modulating that effectiveness.

The portions of the experimental database, however scant, that move beyond internal validity issues to demonstrate ecological validity show that it is possible to produce meaningful change under more naturalistic conditions. The question then becomes how best to extend the database under naturalistic conditions. For this, one must turn to an examination of some of the excluded research articles that we will review shortly. At this point in the development of the field, it is clear that more controlled experimental research in community settings is a legitimate future direction for the extension of PBS.

The nonresearch literature that focuses on consumer needs and interests helps to clarify the gap between the research literature (both included and excluded studies) and what key consumers value, thereby providing a heuristic for moving beyond what researchers presently offer.

In sum, the biases in the database serve a useful function in establishing a trustworthy foundation which, together with the heuristic elements inherent in the excluded research articles and nonresearch literature, provide direction for the further development of the PBS approach.

Is Rigor Over Relevance the Only Choice?

With respect to whether one must choose between rigor and relevance, thoughtful consideration suggests that this issue needs to be restated. Specifically, there is no absolute standard for rigor. Rigor is a function of context. Currently the "gold standard" for rigor is the laboratory experiment, but, as we have seen, this standard is generally unrealistic in complex community settings.

Rigor needs to be defined in terms of its contextual parameters. Analog demonstrations ought to be subjected to criteria for rigor that characterize laboratory research, in which there is an emphasis on highly controlled situations that permit cause and effect statements. In contrast, applied community demonstrations ought to be subjected to criteria for rigor that reflect the realities of carrying out research in situations that typically offer fewer opportunities for manipulating one variable at a time, that frequently contain multiple interacting variables, that require nonresearchers/ nonexperts to implement assessment and intervention, that demand that intervention be conducted over protracted periods of time, and that entail altering social systems to produce validated lifestyle change.

These applied community criteria for rigor have not been systematically articulated in the literature, and, therefore, represent an evolving feature of the field, one that, at its heart, is tantamount to developing a new applied science. From a researcher's perspective, this task represents the greatest challenge offered by the PBS approach.

It is important to note that the laboratory-style experiment remains the only method for determining, definitively, cause and effect relationships. In this case, advances in basic knowledge will still depend on using some variant of the traditional experiment. However, multidimensional projects that focus on intervention efficacy need to be evaluated as well, and, although they may not produce new basic knowledge, they generate a type of applied knowledge that is crucial to advancing the practice of PBS in naturalistic contexts. Some of the research articles excluded from our database represent an important step in moving beyond the current bias favoring experimental studies, and toward incorporating the best information generated by those studies into a research style that focuses on issues of external validity.

External Validity of Excluded Studies

Of the 107 articles excluded for one or more methodological reasons, a number were noteworthy in that they demonstrated the viability of PBS in meeting important criteria for external validity (e.g., Cameron, Ainsleigh, & Bird, 1992; Dadson & Horner, 1993; Horner, Close et al., 1996; Horner, Vaughn, Day, & Ard, 1996; Lucyshyn, Olson, & Horner, 1995; Malette et al., 1992; Northup et al., 1994; Smith, 1985; Smith & Coleman, 1986). Although we did not examine this literature using the detailed analyses applied to the included studies, it may be helpful here to review one representative study that reflects a concern with external validity criteria.

One illustrative study by Horner, Close et al. (1996) involved PBS intervention for 12 adults who had been institutionalized for many years. These individuals were identified by staff as among the most challenging in the entire institution. The approach taken involved a number of PBS interventions whose internal validity had been well established in numerous experimental studies of the type included in our database. Thus, the intervention adopted was built on a solid foundation of experimental research. Importantly, however, numerous variables associated with external validity concerns were combined with the core interventions in order to produce an approach that proved viable in addressing the wider needs of the individuals involved. Specifically, the entire intervention was implemented by typical intervention agents (support staff) rather than by experts or researchers. A supported living model was put in place that focused exclusively on home and community (typical settings) as the site of intervention. Evaluation occurred over a period of 4 years (long-term maintenance). Because of the changing nature of the living situation, repeated assessments were routinely conducted, and intervention was carried out in all relevant contexts. As the natural contexts involved

multivariate control of problem behavior, the intervention itself was multicomponent and included reorganizing the environment (rearranging the physical setting and schedules), changing task features, teaching new skills, altering reinforcing consequences for positive behavior as well as applying extinction to problem behavior, and enhancing health and safety factors. The results of this comprehensive PBS strategy demonstrated decreases in major problem behaviors, greater physical and social inclusion, and stability or improvement in health and safety. Further, both families and direct support staff validated these changes with respect to variables that included community integration, social relationships, problem behavior, and overall quality of life. Thus, validated lifestyle change was evident.

This study, like the others cited earlier, is instructive for two reasons. First, it demonstrates that a comprehensive PBS approach that is responsive to external validity concerns can yield improvements in problem behavior while producing validated lifestyle change. Second, it demonstrates the need to consider anew how we define rigorous applied science; if we do not, we will continue to underestimate the scope and value of PBS applications in community contexts. It is encouraging to note that emerging research addresses the issue of what constitutes rigorous community-based science (e.g., Lucyshyn, Albin, & Nixon, 1997). It is becoming clear that such research will almost certainly need to redefine what is acceptable in the domains of assessment, intervention, and outcomes, a point to which we shall return later.

At this point, it is useful to examine various features of the database while keeping in mind the external validity criteria we have just discussed. In this manner, gaps in the field can begin to be identified and then elaborated upon in the final section of the discussion that deals with the differing perspectives and needs of consumers (nonresearchers).

Drawing Inferences from the Results

In this section, we use the database in order to address the first four research questions posed earlier.

How Widely Applicable Is PBS?

Several researchers have raised the legitimate question of whether PBS might be limited in the scope of its applicability. Specifically, they have cautioned that the approach has, in the past, often focused on individuals who are relatively easy to deal with because they are young and have minor disabilities, high levels of cognitive functioning, and mild problem behavior (Axelrod, 1987; Feldman, 1990; Mulick & Linscheid, 1988). The present data (Table 4) make clear, however, that the field has developed to the point that difficult cases are now being addressed. Thus, (a) over half the cases in our database were adolescents or adults; (b) serious disabilities (i.e., mental retardation, autism) were well represented; (c) fully two-thirds of the cases fell within the severe/profound level of retardation; and (d) the types of problem behavior involved were among the most serious ones seen clinically (aggression, self-injury). There is, however, one area where the scope of applicability of PBS is as yet unclear, specifically, cultural diversity. Very few studies mention minority status as a participant characteristic. More significantly, no studies

investigated whether cultural parameters influenced the design of the PBS approach used. Yet cultural factors have been identified as one important aspect of planning interventions for people with disabilities (Harry, Allen, & McClaughlin, 1995; Harry, Grenot-Scheyer et al., 1995). The systematic exploration of cultural factors and PBS use is a topic that awaits research scrutiny.

Another concern is that the putative complexity of PBS may preempt its applicability to natural (typical) settings unless there is extensive involvement of highly trained professionals (Paisey, Whitney, & Hislop, 1990). Again, however, the data (Table 4) show that almost half of the intervention agents were not experts; they were parents, teachers, job coaches, and the like (typical agents). Further, in one-third of the cases, intervention took place in typical settings (homes, integrated schools), thereby demonstrating that the use of PBS was not restricted to the kinds of specialized settings (e.g., clinics, segregated schools) normally associated with expert professionals.

In What Ways Is the Field Evolving?

General Status of PBS

Historically, the field of developmental disabilities has shown a tendency to embrace new intervention approaches with great enthusiasm and then abandon them with equal enthusiasm as the initial promise of the interventions failed to survive scientific scrutiny (Arendt, MacLean, & Baumeister, 1988; Green & Shane, 1994; Willemsen-Swinkels, Buitelaar, Nijhof, & van Engeland, 1995). Is PBS yet another passing fad? The data (Figure 1) suggest that this approach is here to stay. Over the 12-year period of the review, there was a clear increase in the number of articles published as well as the number of participants and outcomes involved. This increase is especially noteworthy in view of periodic criticisms of PBS alluded to earlier in this review (e.g., see Repp & Singh, 1990).

Demographics

PBS procedures have remained widely applicable over time to individuals with significant problem behavior (Figures 2-6). During the 12-year period reviewed, very young children (preschool age) made up only a small percentage of the cases; most individuals who participated in PBS interventions were older (elementary-school age to adult) and, therefore, presumably more difficult to deal with. Likewise, people diagnosed as having mental retardation or autism, and those with cognitive functioning in the profound or severe range were present in substantial and stable numbers over time, again attesting to the continued applicability of PBS to individuals who are generally viewed as providing serious challenges. Importantly, while the proportion of cases involving aggressive behavior remained stable, those involving dangerous self-injurious behavior and multiple problem behaviors (combinations) actually increased over time. In sum, then, PBS procedures continued to be applied to populations of people who are generally viewed as posing the greatest challenges.

As noted previously, there has been some concern in the field that PBS procedures are being implemented primarily by highly trained experts (atypical intervention agents) in highly specialized (atypical) settings (Paisey et al., 1990; Scotti et al., 1996). Our database

(Figure 7) demonstrated no clear trend with respect to type of intervention agent. Interestingly though, in the last time block (1993-1996), there were equal numbers of typical and atypical intervention agents, a fact that showed the continued heavy involvement of typical intervention agents at a time when the number of PBS studies rose dramatically. Just as important, there appears to be a clear trend in the field toward applying PBS more often in typical settings. Thus, the ratio of typical to atypical settings has, over time, been approaching parity (Figure 8). The field appears to be moving tentatively toward greater use of PBS in natural contexts.

Assessment

For many years, investigators have stressed the importance of conducting an assessment prior to designing an intervention, but they have also noted the relative lack of such assessment in the published literature (Carr et al., 1990; Scotti et al., 1991). More recently, reviews of the entire spectrum of interventions for problem behavior have detected a clear movement toward greater use of assessment methods (Scotti et al., 1996; Didden et al., 1997). Our database confirms that these general trends in the field are seen also in the PBS literature. There has been a dramatic increase over time in the proportion of outcomes associated with prior assessment (Figure 9). To extend previous reviews, we broke down the information obtained so that we could examine trends with respect to specific types of assessment (Figure 10). We found large increases in the use of functional analysis and combinations of assessment procedures. The sole use of indirect or direct observation remained a rarity. Our data also showed that functional analysis was most likely to be associated with atypical intervention agents, atypical settings, and a lack of intervention in all relevant contexts, all indices of lower ecological validity. In contrast, informal and/or direct observation were generally associated with higher levels of ecological validity.

These data suggest that functional analysis is unlikely to be viewed as a feasible method of assessment by practitioners operating in naturalistic contexts. One recent survey (Desrochers, Hile, & Williams-Moseley, 1997) supports this notion. Specifically, 300 practitioners were asked to rank the degree of usefulness of a number of assessment procedures. ABC (antecedent-behavior-consequences) analysis (i.e., a direct observation procedure) and interview with staff/relatives (i.e., an indirect observation procedure) ranked first and second respectively. Functional analysis ranked a very distant fifth in usefulness. Practitioners felt that a lack of environmental control, insufficient time, difficulty collecting data, lack of expertise, and environmental complexity all made functional analysis an impractical and, therefore, seldom used method in real-life settings. Taken as a whole, these considerations argue for the development and refinement of a new generation of nonexperimental assessment procedures that are user-friendly, practical, and feasible, while retaining functional analysis primarily as a tool for researchers and occasionally to be used by experts for cases in which less formal methods have failed. There is, of course, a related strong need for personnel preparation programs and associated texts (e.g., Snell, 1993) that can assist future professionals in conducting valid and practical assessments.

Our review of the PBS literature is also in accord with analyses of motivation documenting that escape is the single most commonly identified function for problem behavior (Scotti et al., 1996). In addition, our database shows that this feature is stable in that escape was associated with the greatest number of outcomes in each successive time block (Figure 11). These data may reflect the decreasing emphasis in the field on custodial care and a greater emphasis on education, involvement in meaningful activities, and work (Emerson et al., 1994). Because escape-motivated problem behavior typically occurs in response to demands (e.g., academic tasks, home chores, work activities), the shift from low-demand custodial situations to higher-demand school and community-based situations may have provided many more opportunities for escape-motivated problem behavior to manifest itself.

Interestingly, the proportion of outcomes involving multiple motivations is accelerating over time. The greater involvement of people with disabilities in typical settings, noted earlier, may be related to the increase in outcomes associated with multiple motivation; the complexity of school, work, and home situations (typical settings) compared to the more restricted, less complex atypical settings may provide increased opportunities for multiple factors (e.g., escape, attention, tangibles) to exert their influence on problem behavior.

The data on whether assessment was repeated provide some important insights on how the field is progressing. Thus, although repeated assessment was associated with only 11 outcomes, 10 of these occurred in the most recent time block. Significantly, repeated assessment was most likely to be carried out in typical settings and by typical intervention agents. In contrast, a lack of repeated assessment was most likely to be associated with atypical agents and atypical settings. These findings make sense given recommendations that assessment should be repeated whenever there are important changes in an individual's life situation (Carr et al., 1994; O'Neill et al., 1997a & b). In typical settings (e.g., home, school), ongoing change is the norm; in atypical settings, ongoing change may be less of a factor, because such settings are often more restricted in terms of activity schedules, social relationships, and reinforcer accessibility. Although the 2:1 ratio of atypical to typical settings seen in the database (Table 4) is consistent with the lopsided ratio of nonrepeated assessment to repeated assessment, the extremely low frequency of the latter does nonetheless represent a relative shortcoming of the field with respect to embracing one standard of best practice.

Intervention

The data (Figure 12) show that both stimulus-based and reinforcement-based interventions have remained an enduring feature of the field. However, there has been an important change toward a predominance of stimulus-based procedures. This change likely reflects a surge of interest, more generally in the field, in making education a priority for people with disabilities. Educationally relevant and popular procedures, such as interspersal training, choice, curricular modification, errorless learning, and prompting, are all stimulus-based and integral to the promotion of learning in academic and related contexts (Luiselli & Cameron, 1998).

As noted earlier, the PBS philosophy does not view people with disabilities as being passive recipients of intervention

for problem behavior. Instead, they are seen as participating in systems that precipitate problem behaviors, and such systems are in need of change.

The data on systems change (Figure 13) suggest a dramatic increase over time in the requirement for behavior change on the part of significant others. Caregivers and support persons are most recently (1993-1996) frequently required to change aspects of their own behavior as one component of intervention. This finding reflects the reciprocity of behavior change that is one hallmark of PBS intervention.

In contrast, the data on environmental reorganization, an additional aspect of systems change, fail to show an increasing trend but remain at low levels. This finding may reflect the abiding predominance of atypical settings over typical settings (Figure 8) as the site for intervention. In typical settings, a major priority is commonly given to selecting engaging activities, enriching lifestyle through community integration, providing choice, systematically providing respite services, and offering other opportunities related to broad environmental reorganization/restructuring (Emerson et al., 1994). Atypical settings are very often more restrictive and institutional, limiting opportunities for such types of broad change. Thus, the imbalance that favors the use of atypical settings over typical settings likely contributed greatly to the lack of focus on environmental reorganization characterizing the current database. The accelerating interest in using typical settings as well as the current paucity of data on environmental reorganization should, together, prompt the field to explore and analyze this aspect of systems change further as one more element of best practice.

Some of what has just been discussed also bears on the finding that the application of intervention in all relevant contexts was uncommon (Figure 14). Further analyses demonstrated that intervention in all relevant contexts was most likely to be associated with typical agents and settings, and least likely with atypical agents and settings. Other data showed that intervention in all relevant contexts was closely associated with combined interventions (i.e., stimulus-based plus reinforcement-based), whereas its absence was closely associated with the use of single interventions (i.e., either stimulus-based or reinforcement-based). One explanation is that atypical agents and settings are often used in analog (laboratory-style) research designed to study basic principles rather than to demonstrate broad clinical changes; so the scope of such interventions may be quite limited (i.e., not all relevant contexts are involved and single interventions are common). In contrast, with typical agents and settings, the focus is often on demonstrating and evaluating the use of interventions across all pertinent aspects of an individual's life, so such interventions may more likely involve all relevant contexts and the application of combined interventions. The paucity of data on intervention in all relevant contexts may reflect a strong interest, at least in the literature sample reviewed, in elucidating basic principles at the expense of demonstrating broad-spectrum behavior change. Because the latter activity is at least as important as the former, one priority for the field would be to redress this imbalance.

The pattern we have been describing, involving typical versus atypical agents and settings, is seen once again in the analysis of combined interventions (i.e., those involving both stimulus-based and reinforcement-based as part of the same intervention package). Figure 12 shows no trend for the increased or decreased use of combined interventions. However, additional analyses make clear that combined interventions, when they did occur, were more likely to be conducted by typical intervention agents and in typical settings. Noncombined interventions were more likely to be conducted by atypical agents and in atypical settings. This pattern also conforms to the distinction between analog research and applied research in the community. In the former type of laboratory-style research, one typically avoids combining multiple variables, favoring instead the manipulation of as few variables as possible to demonstrate cause-and-effect relationships unambiguously. In contrast, the latter type of research is more concerned with demonstrating the efficacy of intervention packages (i.e., the most potent combination of interventions).

In sum, then, the data in Figures 12–14 yield a fairly consistent picture in terms of the very different research and clinical agenda represented by typical agents working in typical settings versus atypical agents working in atypical settings.

A final aspect of the intervention data pertains to the use of non-PBS procedures (Figure 12). These procedures were much less frequently used than PBS throughout the entire time period reviewed. This finding implies that, for a clear majority of outcomes, PBS by itself was viewed by investigators as an adequate approach for dealing with serious problem behavior; the addition of non-PBS procedures was not seen as a necessity. Subsequent analyses, discussed shortly, corroborate and amplify this conclusion.

Outcomes

For many years, PBS advocates, among others, have argued strongly that reduction in problem behavior is an insufficient outcome unless such reduction is associated with broader changes that include stimulus and response generalization, maintenance, and improvements in lifestyle (Carr et al., 1994; Horner, Dunlap, & Koegel, 1988; Koegel et al., 1996; Meyer & Evans, 1989; Schalock, 1990; Turnbull & Turnbull, 1996). Our database (Figure 15) suggests that this call for best practices has gone largely unheeded. Relatively few outcomes involved demonstrations of broad change. Thus, no trends were seen for stimulus generalization and only a small increase was seen for response generalization. Demonstrations of short-term maintenance (less than 6 months) became more frequent over the period reviewed; however, demonstrations of longer-term maintenance dropped sharply in frequency as the duration of follow-up was extended. Significantly, no outcomes were tracked for more than 2 years, thus leaving unanswered the question of whether PBS can produce permanent change. Of most concern, however, is the finding that a focus on lifestyle change was uncommon, with no compelling upward trend. Studies meeting our rigorous inclusion criteria appeared more concerned with demonstrating initial efficacy and with understanding of process, and less concerned with more generalized change including improvements in lifestyle. This gap in the literature helps define a critical research priority for the future.

The lack of focus on broad change is paralleled by a lack of focus on social validity (Figure 16). Social validity data were available for only a small number of outcomes. Modest increases over time were seen for questions dealing with the feasibility of intervention and the acceptability of intervention outcomes, but no trends were seen for questions pertaining to the desirability of specific intervention procedures and the effectiveness of intervention in producing lifestyle change. The paucity of data on social validation may be linked to the paucity of data on broad change. That is, to the extent that investigators have been largely concerned with demonstrating intervention effects in somewhat circumscribed contexts, it makes little sense to ask social validity questions that are intended to tap consumer satisfaction across a broad range of circumstances. A greater future emphasis on studies of broad behavior change should lead as well to a greater focus on whether such change is socially valid.

How Effective Is PBS?

Changes in Positive Behavior

Our database (Figure 17) documented, true to the definition of PBS, increases in positive behavior. Data available for slightly less than half the outcomes demonstrated modest to substantial increases in socially desirable responses (positive behaviors) as a consequence of intervention. These data are important because they show that the field has moved beyond an exclusive concern with reducing problem behavior per se and has become more committed to enhancing constructive aspects of individuals' repertoires as a general strategy for dealing with problem behavior.

Distribution of Outcome Effectiveness: What Constitutes a Success?

There were many instances in which PBS was an effective strategy for reducing the level of serious problem behavior (Table 5). The two generic variations of PBS, stimulus-based and reinforcement-based, were about equally effective in producing successful outcomes (Tables 5 & 6). It is important to understand, however, that the field has not yet reached a consensus on what constitutes a success. As can be noted in the distribution of outcome effectiveness (Table 5), the degree of success depends on where one sets the cutoff criterion. Across all PBS-based outcomes, a criterion of 100% reduction (total elimination of problem behavior) produced a success rate of 26.8%, one quarter of all the outcomes. Few investigators set so demanding a criterion. Instead, in the present paper, as well as in the earlier review the senior author conducted for the National Institutes of Health (Carr et al., 1990), a 90% or more reduction criterion was established that yielded a success rate of 51.6%, one half of all the outcomes. Other investigators (Mulick & Kedesdy, 1988) have used an 80% or more reduction criterion, which in the present case would produce a success rate of 68.0%, two thirds of all the outcomes. An 80% reduction criterion might, at first glance, appear unacceptably low. Yet clinically, if an individual who has been biting him- or herself an average of 100 times a day for many months were to decrease biting abruptly to 20 times a day, caregivers might rate the outcome as a qualified success. In contrast, even a 90% reduction in a less challenging self-injurious behavior (e.g., trichotillomania: hair pulling) might be viewed as unimpressive and relatively

unsuccessful. The point is that other variables besides percentage reduction contribute to the definition of intervention success. In this vein, the many demonstrations in the literature of dramatic decreases in problem behavior during 10-minute analog sessions conducted by researchers are not, a priori, superior to more modest decreases reported for interventions applied throughout the day in natural settings by typical caregivers, a serious concern that needs more systematic attention in the future.

Table 5 also shows that for 33 outcomes (9% of the total), problem behavior decreased minimally (only 0-19% from baseline) or increased. Our previous review (Carr et al., 1990) likewise noted negative outcomes in a small minority of cases. Such findings serve to underscore the point that no intervention, including PBS, should be assumed to be universally effective. As noted later, negative outcomes may reflect the influence of variables (e.g., non-optimal social systems, physiological factors) that attenuate the impact of PBS strategies. Identifying such variables represents yet another research priority for the field.

Success Rates Pooled Across Outcomes

With all the caveats just discussed in mind, we used a 90% reduction criterion as our definition of success. Using this criterion, it was clear (Table 6) that the success rate was invariant and not dependant on the type of intervention employed. Generally, about half the outcomes could be categorized as successes, irrespective of whether they were associated with stimulus-based or reinforcement-based intervention and/or different combinations of these with non-PBS procedures. However, further analyses of these data highlight some of the complexities that are not initially apparent from examination of Table 6 alone.

Single Versus Multiple Interventions

The fact that single interventions had a success rate of 51.5%, and combination interventions had a success rate of 52.4%, might make it appear as if not much is gained by combining stimulus-based and reinforcement-based intervention into a comprehensive approach. However, as noted earlier, single interventions were most likely to be carried out by atypical agents (e.g., research psychologists) in atypical settings (e.g., institutions) whereas combined interventions were most likely to be carried out by typical agents (e.g., parents) in typical settings (e.g., homes). The degree of control available in typical settings involving typical agents is, arguably, substantially less than that achievable by experts (atypical agents) operating in more restricted (atypical) settings. Therefore, one might expect poorer outcomes associated with the former as compared to the latter. Because this result was not the case (i.e., the success rates were about the same), one could conclude that combined intervention might be particularly useful in dealing with situations in which natural (typical) intervention agents must address the day-to-day (typical) settings in which many people with disabilities live.

The Role of Consequences

Whereas PBS interventions are proactive (i.e., take place in the absence of problem behavior and act to prevent future occurrences of such behavior), non-PBS interventions are reactive (i.e., take place at the moment problem behavior is occurring and act as direct consequences for such behavior). The data (Table 6) suggest that non-PBS interventions that stress consequences may not always be necessary for dealing with problem behavior because (a) for almost three quarters of the database (72.1% of the outcomes), PBS procedures were used alone and (b) the rate of success was virtually the same with or without non-PBS (i.e., 51.5% successes with PBS alone, and 52.0% with non-PBS). Again, however, consideration of a number of factors suggests that this conclusion needs to be tempered and qualified. Here we will discuss two key factors, the role of punishment and extinction as response consequences.

Punishment: A Form of Crisis Management

Most practitioners and caregivers are concerned about what they can do at the moment of crisis, when dangerous behavior is occurring, to mitigate its effects. Our database (Table 7) shows that approximately half of the non-PBS interventions took the form of punishment, albeit, with one exception (water mist), punishments that are usually regarded as relatively nonintrusive. The fact that generally innocuous non-PBS procedures (added to the PBS procedures already in place) were sufficient without the addition of more highly intrusive procedures should be encouraging to those opposed to the use of the latter more controversial measures. As has been pointed out elsewhere (Carr et al., 1994), intervention agents frequently feel the need for crisis management procedures even when committed to a PBS approach. The perceived need for these procedures cannot easily be dismissed. The important message from our database, however, is that when additional non-PBS procedures seemed necessary, they were relatively benign, and relatively rare.

Extinction: A Crucial Consequence?

Our database (Table 7) also showed that approximately half of the non-PBS interventions took the form of extinction. There are conceptual grounds for assuming that extinction may not always be necessary, but there are additional grounds that support its use. Conceptually, both the Matching Law and the notion of response efficiency may plausibly obviate the use of extinction. The Matching Law states that the relative rate of a response is a function of the relative rate of reinforcement for that response (McDowell, 1982). Thus, if an individual receives all his or her reinforcement contingent on aggressive behavior, that behavior would occur at a high frequency. But suppose, through PBS intervention, the individual acquired many new skills (responses) that also provided access to reinforcement. Now this person would not be solely dependent on aggression as a means for accessing reinforcers. Thus, even if aggressive behavior were reinforced at the same level as it had been prior to PBS intervention, the relative rate of this behavior would now be much lower because of the presence of many new skills (responses) that generate additional reinforcement. So the absence of an extinction contingency for aggressive behavior would not necessarily matter, because many available competing positive responses reduced the relative rate of reinforcement for aggression with the result that aggression would now be less frequent.

Response efficiency is another factor. Data show that if two responses both

access the same reinforcer, the more efficient of the two is likely to predominate (Horner & Day, 1991). Let us say an individual acquired a new response (e.g., communication) as a result of PBS intervention. But then the individual continued to receive reinforcement for aggressive behavior (i.e., no extinction contingency). If the new response was more efficient than the aggressive behavior, the new response would predominate, and aggression would become less frequent.

The possible role of the Matching Law and response efficiency in decreasing incidents of problem behavior in the absence of extinction may explain why so few outcomes in the database were associated with the use of extinction. Investigators may simply have found it to be unnecessary. Nonetheless, a variety of considerations support its use. First, many investigators, while not providing formal data on the use of extinction, made passing references to "ignoring" problem behavior or "not rewarding" it, both statements implying that some degree of extinction was in effect. Thus, the number of outcomes associated with extinction (Table 7) may represent an underestimate. Second, and more critically, the Matching Law itself suggests why extinction may be important. Specifically, if in addition to strengthening new skills that access the reinforcers previously associated with problem behavior alone, one were also to discontinue the reinforcement of the problem behavior itself (extinction), then one would be greatly increasing the relative rate of reinforcement for the new (positive) skills. This strategy would also have the effect of increasing the relative frequency of positive behavior. In this crucial respect, extinction could, on conceptual grounds, be viewed as an important procedure because it directly potentiates the display of positive behavior. On these grounds alone, it would be prudent to include extinction as part of any PBS-based approach.

Stimulus Generalization, Response Generalization, and Maintenance

These three measures of generalization were typically associated with small numbers of outcomes. Yet, with a 90% reduction criterion for problem behavior, about two-thirds of the outcomes were successes for stimulus generalization and for the various durations of maintenance. Response generalization was much less successful, with small gains in appropriate behavior characteristic of most of the outcomes. The scant attention paid to these three measures of generalization was criticized in our earlier review of PBS intervention (Carr et al., 1990). Unfortunately, this gap in best practices remains an enduring feature of the field; there remains a strong bias toward demonstrating experimental control of problem behavior in restricted situations rather than investigating more widespread change.

Full implementation of the PBS approach would significantly increase the database pertinent to generalization measures. Specifically, a greater focus on assessing and remediating problem behavior in all relevant contexts (not just analog settings) would, of necessity, teach specific alternatives to problem behavior in many different situations (multiple exemplar training), a factor known to promote stimulus generalization (Stokes & Baer, 1977). Likewise, extensive assessment and intervention for deficient

behavior repertoires would teach and strengthen a wide variety of responses (communication, self-management, social skills) whose increase might well change many other behaviors in a response generalization paradigm (Carr, 1988). Finally, because optimum PBS intervention is not saltatory but, rather, continuous, ongoing, and permanent, maintenance is potentially a natural consequence of the approach. To state the matter differently, the hallmark of the PBS philosophy is to remediate deficiencies in all contexts (i.e., deficient environments and deficient skill repertoires). Once this remediation has occurred, agents take steps to ensure that the contexts do not deteriorate to their initial levels of deficiency. In this manner, maintenance is promoted indefinitely.

Lifestyle Change and Social Validity

The ultimate goals of PBS intervention are to enable individuals to live more normalized lives (lifestyle change) and to have key consumers (e.g., caregivers, support persons, and, if possible, the people with disabilities themselves) agree that the intervention and its effects are worthwhile (social validity). A strong movement developing in the field emphasizes the centrality of these goals in service provision and remediation efforts (Dennis, Williams, Giangreco, & Cloninger, 1993; Hughes, Hwang, Kim, Eisenman, & Killian, 1995; Risley, 1996; Sands, Kozleski, & Goodwin, 1991; Schalock, 1990, 1996; Turnbull & Turnbull, 1996). Yet the database does not reflect this emphasis. Specifically, only a small number of outcomes focused on these issues. Data on successful lifestyle change were taken on only 8 out of the

230 participants in our sample, and these successful outcomes were partially validated by a likewise small sample of consumers, none of whom was an actual participant. Clearly, a large gap exists between the stated goals for PBS intervention and the intensive and systematic empirical exploration of these goals.

Several factors have hindered the development of a larger database. First, as noted earlier, our rigorous inclusion criteria resulted in the elimination of a number of studies (on methodological grounds) that did demonstrate validated lifestyle change. The interpretability of these studies was problematic, however, primarily because the standard of rigor that exists in many parts of the field emphasizes a degree of experimental control that is most easily achieved in analog situations. Perhaps that is why so many outcomes were associated with restricted (atypical) settings in which the intervention was carried out by expert (atypical) intervention agents in restricted circumstances (i.e., not all relevant contexts). Tightly controlling the context in this manner greatly increases the prospects of achieving internal validity but does so at the expense of developing a truly applied technology that has the multidimensional properties needed for addressing goals larger than experimental control, namely, validated lifestyle change. As noted previously, rigor is not an absolute construct but, rather, a function of context. Thus, the standards defining rigor for analog studies that stress the analysis of process will almost certainly have to be different from the standards defining rigor for naturalistic, community-based studies that stress the analysis of outcome.

What Factors Modulate the Effectiveness of PBS?

Demographic Variables

Although success rates varied within many of the demographic variables (e.g., on the age variable, success rates were considerably higher for adolescents than for adults), comparison of the present database (Table 10) with that obtained in previous related reviews (e.g., Carr et al., 1990; Scotti et al., 1991) does not reveal any replicated trends. One could not conclude, for instance, that problem behavior in adults is consistently more difficult to remediate than problem behavior in adolescents. In addition, the literature contains no conceptual basis for inferring that variations in demographic variables, such as gender, age, diagnosis, retardation level, or topography (type) of problem behavior, ought to bear a systematic relationship to intervention success.

We intentionally included an additional variable not explored in previous reviews: the relative difficulty in dealing with single types of problem behavior versus combinations of types. Data indicated that the latter was associated with lower success rates; this may be due in part to the increased challenge of intervening on multiple types of problem behavior. It may be that multiple problem behaviors serve multiple functions, thereby requiring the design of interventions that are more complex and, therefore, more prone to failure. Alternatively, the great effort required to deal with diverse problem behavior may render support people less likely to persevere in intervention efforts, resulting in poor outcomes. In any case, the analysis of single versus combination problem behavior has not been adequately explored in the literature; the possibility that this factor may modulate intervention effectiveness makes it worthy of study.

Influence of Assessment Variables

One of the most striking findings was that the success rate for interventions based on some form of functional assessment was almost twice that of interventions not based on a prior assessment (Table 11). This finding appears robust, having been noted also in several previous reviews (Carr et al., 1990; Didden et al., 1997; Scotti et al., 1991). The relationship between assessment and successful outcomes suggests that the field needs to develop assessment technology further; as noted, the predominant tool is currently functional analysis, and this type of assessment requires a level of expertise and a degree of experimental control that is frequently absent in community-based settings involving typical intervention agents. We return to this point when we consider what gaps in knowledge exist in the field and how best to address them.

With respect to type of function, it was clear that outcome success was uniformly substantial (i.e., an approximately 60% success rate) across the various functions with one notable exception: The sensory function was associated with an extremely low success rate. Although this finding might simply reflect sampling error based on the small number of outcomes associated with the sensory function, there is a noteworthy alternative explanation. Specifically, all the other functions were socially mediated; the sensory function was not. One

interpretation of this finding is that PBS intervention is not pertinent to problem behavior that lacks social mediation. A more optimistic interpretation is that the field has not as yet adequately addressed nonsocially mediated problem behavior within a PBS framework; if it were to do so, success rates would rise. Certainly, there are instances of problem behavior related to physiological variables that would logically appear to be outside the purview of a PBS approach (Gardner & Whalen, 1996; Guess & Siegel-Causey, 1995; Lowry & Sovner, 1992; Schroeder & Tessel, 1994). For example, it has been known for some time that certain genetic conditions such as Lesch-Nyhan syndrome may cause self-injurious behavior (Seegmiller, 1972). Whether sensory-based behavior is likewise outside the PBS approach is currently an empirical question. One working hypothesis postulates that extending PBS interventions so as to provide nonproblem-behavior alternatives for accessing relevant sensory stimuli might undermine sensory-based problem behavior, thereby improving success rates (Favell et al., 1982; Prosser, 1988; Smith, 1986).

Finally, the small sample of outcomes associated with repeated assessment is not in keeping with best practices. If PBS is truly an approach designed to deal with problem behavior across all relevant contexts for protracted periods of time, it strains credibility to believe that a single assessment would suffice to understand the totality of problem behavior across changing circumstances over many years. One interpretation of the relatively low success rate associated with repeated assessment is that the field has not yet explored this issue with the same intensity and detail as it has explored the issue of short-term analog assessment in restricted settings. Developing a larger database on this topic could help identify and refine the factors critical for ensuring meaningful repeated assessment.

Systems Change

Recall that a critical aspect of PBS intervention is the remediation of deficient contexts in an effort to normalize them. This requires change in systems and not just in the person with disabilities. The data (Table 12) show that change in the behavior of significant others was frequent and associated with success rates higher than when the significant others were not required to alter their behavior. One mechanism related to this greater success may involve the degree of support the significant others provide for newly enhanced skills displayed by the person with disabilities. Thus, if the person with disabilities begins to use communication rather than problem behavior as a way of accessing attention, then greater responsivity to bids for attention ensures that the new communicative behavior will be strengthened and better able to compete with problem behavior. Likewise, being able to "read" when a person with disabilities is seeking attention nonverbally (e.g., via furtive glances toward the significant other) and then responding to these nonverbal cues prior to the display of problem behavior represents another change in behavior that serves, in this instance, to prevent further display of problem behavior. The type and magnitude of behavior change shown by significant others as well as their relation to intervention success have been studied only minimally in the literature. Our database implies that it would be fruitful to explore such change further by focusing on issues of reciprocity (i.e., both parties in a social exchange alter their behavior) rather than the more traditional emphasis on unilateral strategies (i.e., only the person with the problem behavior is the focus of intervention, and the primary goal is for that person to change).

The data on environmental reorganization, though scant, suggest that this molar approach can produce higher success rates than those approaches from which it is excluded or minimized. Here the effective mechanism may relate to the fact that broad environmental change (e.g., altering personnel, reorganizing activity schedules, changing the physical properties of the home and/or school) often provides an array of discriminative stimuli and setting events that potentiate the display of positive behaviors (Carr, Carlson, Langdon, Magito-McLaughlin, & Yarbrough, 1998) that, in turn, compete with the problem behavior. Importantly, our earlier discussion noted that our database includes a preponderance of atypical settings involving atypical intervention agents who fail to address problem behavior in all relevant contexts. This fact may account for the small database related to environmental reorganization, because any approach that minimizes naturalistic variables simultaneously limits the scope of opportunities available for instituting molar systems change. The solution to this dilemma lies in new research priorities that stress the inclusion of naturalistic variables the presence of which would motivate researchers to analyze and evaluate broad environmental change. The conceptual underpinnings for this expanded approach are clearly evident in the literature on ecological systems theory (Bronfenbrenner, 1989). This theory is compatible with the operant perspective but also suggests additional useful practices for understanding the individual's behavior in context and for planning interventions oriented toward broad systems change. The developmental literature provides evidence that for parents the ongoing presence of informal social support that includes (a) multiple, high-quality, stable relationships and (b) assistance from members of a broader interpersonal network correlates strongly with parents' viewing their child's behavior as less troublesome or difficult (Dunst, Trivette, & Jodry, 1997). Observations such as these should spur the field into examining problem behavior from the perspective of broader ecological variables.

Ecological Validity

One might anticipate that the higher degree of experimental control that frequently characterizes interventions in restrictive situations (i.e., those involving atypical settings and interventions that do not occur in all relevant contexts) might produce higher success rates, particularly when the intervention agent is an expert/professional. The database (Table 13) does not confirm this expectation. Instead, typical agents are associated with higher success rates. Further, the success rates involving typical versus atypical settings, and the presence versus absence of intervention in all relevant contexts, are roughly comparable. One could argue that atypical agents work with individuals displaying more difficult problem behavior, thus providing an explanation for their lower success rates. However, as there is no consensus in the field as to what metric should be used to gauge level of difficulty, one cannot know whether this interpretation is correct. In addition, it is important to note that when typical agents implemented intervention,

they did so only after they had referred the case to one or more experts/professionals who then helped them structure the intervention. In other words, the atypical agents were still involved albeit in a consultative role rather than as implementors.

It is encouraging that typical intervention agents were able to produce good success rates, as ultimately these are the people who must carry the brunt of intervention in day-to-day situations. It is even more encouraging that the generally less controlled, less restrictive situations represented by typical settings produced success rates comparable to those obtained in atypical settings. Finally, it is most encouraging that intervention in all relevant contexts, truly a best practice, produced success rates at least as good as those obtained with more circumscribed intervention that did not address all relevant contexts. In sum, the ecological data suggest that the involvement of typical intervention agents may increase success rates and that implementing intervention in less restrictive circumstances (i.e., typical settings, all relevant contexts) does not typically decrease the success rate much below the 50% level obtained generally. Apparently, with PBS intervention, it is possible to have both successful outcomes and ecological validity.

Implications for Future Research

We have now reviewed the database for studies that met our methodological criteria for inclusion. Earlier we noted the bias in this database toward articles that emphasized internal validity concerns. Although some portions of the database did address external validity concerns, it was clear that the bulk of the literature emphasizing these concerns is found in the excluded research articles and, to a great extent, among clinical reports and descriptive accounts provided by practitioners, parents, trainers, and others concerned with day-to-day support in naturalistic contexts. In Chapter 1, we alluded to the gap between the needs and interests of researchers and those of nonresearchers (consumers). Having reviewed the database, we are now in a position to weigh its strengths and weaknesses in light of nonresearcher concerns so we can formulate an agenda that addresses knowledge gaps by building on what is known while frankly acknowledging what is not known. This issue, of course, is the basis for the fifth and final research question to which we now turn our attention.

How Responsive Is the PBS Literature to the Needs of Consumers (Nonresearchers)?

Four priorities stand out in the literature as pertaining especially to the needs of consumers: (a) comprehensive lifestyle support, (b) long-term change, (c) practicality and relevance, and (d) consumer support issues. We will examine each of these in turn.

Comprehensive Lifestyle Support

Families and friends of people with developmental disabilities are focused on issues pertaining to family life, jobs, community inclusion, supported living, and expanding social relationships (Risley, 1996; Ruef, 1997; Turnbull & Ruef, 1996, 1997; Turnbull & Turnbull, 1996), in short, comprehensive lifestyle support. The database, as a whole, does not reflect

this priority. First, only a tiny minority of outcomes involved goals of lifestyle change, implementation of lifestyle intervention, or reports of successful lifestyle change (Figure 15). Second, few data were reported on stimulus and response generalization (Table 8), measures that are indicative of broad change. Third, the preponderance of atypical settings (Figure 8), and the relative lack of intervention in all relevant contexts (Figure 14) are not responsive to family perspectives that stress the need for good adjustment to real-life settings and round-the-clock support to achieve this goal. Fourth, the paucity of interventions that combine stimulus-based and reinforcement-based interventions into a comprehensive multicomponent approach (Table 6) also indicates that the emphasis is not on providing interventions that demonstrate efficacy across complex, changing contexts such as those that typify community settings. Fifth, the call for extensive environmental reorganization as a crucial strategy for ensuring improvement in lifestyle (Risley, 1996) has not been heeded. Few outcomes were associated with this type of systems change (Table 12).

Yet the gaps just noted need not remain a permanent feature of the research literature. Even in the current database, there were indications that this situation can improve. However, although they were in the minority, there were demonstrations of successful lifestyle change as well as stimulus and response generalization. Also, some investigators have, with good effect, intervened in all relevant contexts, used combined (multicomponent) interventions, and reorganized environments. There is also a clear trend toward implementing PBS more often in typical settings. Taken as a whole, these data show that it is possible to respond to consumer needs for comprehensive lifestyle change. Indeed, this embryonic research base, when combined with similar information from the excluded research studies as well as numerous reports in the nonresearch literature, fully justifies a major shift in research priorities toward analysis and evaluation of comprehensive lifestyle support. As noted, all the elements of this approach are present in the literature. Generally lacking at the moment are (a) rules for their systematic combination and (b) the scientific scrutiny of those rules that is necessary to prove efficacy.

Long-Term Change

Consumers tend to be concerned about problem behavior over long periods of time. Families note that advocacy efforts necessary to achieve comprehensive lifestyle change can often take years (Nickels, 1996; Turnbull & Turnbull, 1996). Both teachers and families state that transitioning individuals from preschool to elementary and high school and then to the workplace and supported living requires a lifespan perspective that views the successful management of problem behavior as a never-ending process responsive to different challenges at different stages of life (Turnbull, 1988; Vandercook, York, & Forest, 1989). Not surprisingly, then, the overall short-term, uncoordinated nature of programs and supports has all parents, even those who are currently satisfied with their programs, worried about the future (Ruef, 1997; Turnbull & Ruef, 1997). The database reveals a substantial gap between the needs of consumers for long-term demonstrations of efficacy and the interests of researchers who follow individuals for short periods of time, most typically for less than 6 months and

in no case for more than 2 years (Table 9).

There are, however, both empirical and conceptual grounds for believing that the gap can be closed. First, the database includes a limited number of demonstrations of successful maintenance effects lasting up to 2 years. There is no a priori reason for assuming that the effects cannot be further extended, especially given the excluded research studies and clinical reports, some of which note long-term maintenance. At a conceptual level, one might expect long-term effects if the PBS approach were implemented in a manner more consistent with its general philosophy. To the extent that deficient environments and deficient skills continue to be identified over time, which is almost always the case when one follows an individual over many years in changing life circumstances, PBS strategies would have to be added and/or modified. In other words, intervention never stops. This view is in contrast to many traditional studies in which maintenance is defined as durable success following intervention cessation (Carr et al., 1990). In a truly comprehensive PBS approach, maintenance would be guaranteed because intervention would never stop. Interestingly, an added benefit of such a long-term strategy is that, over time, the individual is supported in many different situations (a feature that would enhance stimulus generalization) and is taught many different skills (a feature that would enhance response generalization). Thus, comprehensive changes are likely to be facilitated over the protracted periods of time that PBS is in effect. In short, maintenance and comprehensive lifestyle change are intertwined variables.

Practicality and Relevance

Unless consumers view a research finding as being usable in their particular circumstances, it is unlikely that it will guide day-to-day efforts to effect meaningful, long-term change. The gap between research and practice is highlighted by the fact that researchers generally focus on methodological rigor, whereas consumers generally focus on practicality and relevance (Carnine, 1997).

Both interviews (Turnbull & Ruef, 1996) and focus groups (Ruef, 1997) conducted with families indicate that relevance is most often defined as pertaining to lifestyle change. However, as noted before, this topic is dealt with only marginally in the database. Families are also concerned with a number of practical issues (Ruef, 1997) that go beyond the simple desire for information about the nature of specific interventions: (a) How many people are necessary to implement PBS, and can a parent do it alone? (b) How much training does a parent need, and must one become an expert to be successful? (c) What is the average number of hours per week necessary to effectively implement PBS in the first 6 months? After 6 months? After 1 year? (d) Can one be successful by implementing only part of the PBS approach? (e) Are there shortcuts (e.g., simpler versions of functional assessment), and how does one sustain the energy levels necessary for long-term efforts? (f) How can parents effectively implement PBS when their own fears, embarrassment, and anger get in the way (maintaining composure)? (g) How can parents do an effective job in the face of negative reactions from friends, acquaintances, family, and others in the community? The fact that the database rarely confronts these issues demonstrates the existence of a wide research-to-practice gap that argues in favor of a future research agenda centering on practicality criteria.

With respect to other consumer groups, the issues may vary, but the focus on practicality and relevance does not. Teachers, for example, regard proper training for managing problem behavior as a top priority (Pearman, Huang, & Mellblom, 1997). Again, their concern is not just with the specifics of intervention but, rather, with how well intervention practices will fit into the system in which they work (Ruef, 1997): (a) How can PBS be implemented in a general-education classroom? (b) How does PBS vary as a function of grade level (elementary, middle school, high school)? (c) What structural modifications are required for implementation in special-education versus general-education settings? (d) What systems prerequisites must be satisfied for PBS to be a viable option (e.g., does it matter if you have one child with a disability in a class of typical children or a class composed entirely of children with disabilities)? (e) Does implementing PBS with one student take away time spent with other students (fairness)? The database rarely touches these topics, a fact that is particularly evident from the small number of outcomes associated with broad environmental reorganization, a key facet of systems change (Table 12). That teachers widely perceive research to be irrelevant to their needs is also evident from data showing that fewer than 1% of the nation's 4 million teachers participate in the American Federation of Teachers Education Research and Development program in which emphasis is placed on using research to make informed educational decisions to guide practice (Billups, 1997).

Other groups of consumers such as friends of people with disabilities, policy makers, and people with disabilities themselves raise questions about the complexity of systems change and the relevance of current research for dealing with this complexity (Morrissey, 1997; Ruef, 1997).

Several developments in the field point to a way of closing the research-to-practice gap to enhance practicality and relevance. Specifically the Participatory Action Research (PAR) approach sees researchers and consumers as collaborators (Meyer & Evans, 1993; Turnbull, Friesen, & Ramirez, 1998). Traditionally, researchers have defined the issues, formulated a plan for investigating the issues, and occasionally disseminated the results to consumers (but more often to other researchers). The PAR model, in contrast, views consumers as having an active rather than passive role. Consumers can play many roles that include helping to define the issues, assisting in the design of those aspects of the research that enhance ecological and social validity, and providing consultation on how to package the results so that they are more readily usable by other consumers. Policy makers have called for this type of collaboration for several years now (Lloyd, Weintraub, & Safer, 1997; Malouf & Schiller, 1995). However, with virtually no exceptions, the PAR model was not a feature associated with our database. Nonetheless, it is encouraging to note that in a recent issue of the *Journal of Special Education* devoted to research in severe disabilities, multiple researchers independently endorsed the idea of making the PAR model a critical component of a future research agenda for the field (Browder, 1997; Nietupski, Hamre-Nietupski, Curtin, & Shrikanth, 1997; Reichle, 1997). In sum, although parents and teachers, for example, will typically not have the expertise to enhance the technical design aspects of

research, they can and should play a major role in enhancing ecological and social validity and in identifying and resolving barriers to achieving successful outcomes.

Although the database on social validity was scant (Figure 16), it is somewhat encouraging to note that the data were generally positive with respect to issues of feasibility, desirability, acceptability, and lifestyle change, suggesting that, at least for the limited sample of consumers involved, PBS was viewed as practical and relevant. The field needs to build on this base by developing research models that reflect the major elements of the PAR approach. In this regard, recent work on goodness-of-fit models (Albin, Lucyshyn, Horner, & Flannery, 1996) seem especially relevant. This research strategy stresses the notion that interventions must be congruent with contextual variables involving participant characteristics, characteristics of the people who will be implementing the plan, and systems features related to the environment in which the plan is to be implemented. Consumer needs and priorities are critical. Recent research demonstrates clearly that a focus on goodness-of-fit not only produces socially valued intervention outcomes but is the logical translation of the PAR philosophy into scientific methodology (Lucyshyn et al., 1995, 1997).

Consumers Want Support, Too

It is easy to misinterpret PBS as referring only to the person with disabilities, namely, how best to support that person through skills training, environmental reorganization, and a focus on improving lifestyle. However, as we noted, PBS refers to systems change broadly conceived, that is, all elements of the system including the needs of other people who must support the person with disabilities. Thus, a critical theme that has emerged in the literature is that consumers such as parents and teachers require support.

Some researchers have argued forcefully that professional support should be family-centered and entail comprehensive systems change involving all relevant parties and not just the person with disabilities (Albin et al., 1996; Dunlap & Robbins, 1991). Nonetheless, parents continue to report a lack of family-centered service delivery systems and an overall lack of support from professionals paid to deliver services (Wheeler, 1996). Few examples exist in the literature that demonstrate support for the people (families) who must carry the weight of supporting others (c.f., Lucyshyn et al., 1995, 1997; The Family Connection staff et al., 1996; Turnbull & Turnbull, 1996).

Interestingly, although both parents and teachers value advice and training from professionals, they particularly value parent-to-parent and teacher-to-teacher mentoring (Gersten & Brengelman, 1996; Gersten, Morvant, & Brengelman, 1995; Ruef, 1997; Santelli, Turnbull, Marquis, & Lerner, 1993, 1995). Teachers also value emotional support from principals and other administrators as a way of coping with high job stress in working with challenging populations (Fimian, 1986; Littrell, Billingsley, & Cross, 1994).

In some limited respects, the database touches on several of the concerns just described. Thus, the fact that typical intervention agents working in typical settings are sometimes intervening in all relevant contexts (Table 13) is a step in the right direction, because this pattern implies family-centered and school-centered services. However, as noted previously, this pattern is associated with only a minority of outcomes in the database. More significant perhaps, the database does not show, in any systematic way, a concern for the broader needs of consumers that involves issues such as peer mentoring, emotional support, and stress reduction. Instead, a premium is placed on teaching specific intervention strategies at the expense of a focus on the broader systems issues related to supporting consumers who will be responsible for facilitating lifestyle changes for decades (i.e., parents often do this for 50 or more years, and siblings can have this role for even longer). This gap in the research literature can be addressed only by enlarging the conception of best practices to include the systematic assessment of consumer needs and by acting on those needs by designing supports for the supporters—families, teachers, job coaches, and other community-based staff.

CHAPTER 5
SUMMARY

We now summarize the findings with the greatest clinical and conceptual significance as they relate to the five research questions posed at the beginning of this review.

How Widely Applicable is PBS?

1. The approach is widely applicable to people with serious disabilities who exhibit serious problem behavior.

2. The approach can be applied by typical intervention agents in typical settings. Its use is not restricted to experts operating in specialized circumstances although a majority of outcomes are still associated with this pattern.

In What Ways is the Field Evolving?

1. PBS is not a fad. It has been showing steady and dramatic growth especially over the most recent time period reviewed.

2. Outcomes involving the most difficult problem behavior (e.g., SIB and combinations of problem behaviors) have become more numerous.

3. Generally, typical and atypical intervention agents are about equally likely to conduct PBS intervention. With respect to intervention settings, atypical settings are more likely to be the venue for intervention. However, there is a steady increase over time in the use of typical settings, and the gap between the use of typical versus atypical settings is closing.

4. There has been a dramatic increase over time in the use of assessment prior to planning intervention.

5. Both formal functional analysis and combination assessments have become more numerous. There is concern, however, as to whether functional analysis is a practical method in naturalistic contexts.

6. There is a clear focus on escape-motivated problem behavior and on problem behaviors that are multiply motivated.

7. Repeated assessments have remained uncommon. When they do occur, they are likely to be carried out by typical intervention agents and in typical settings.

8. Stimulus-based intervention has gradually become more common than reinforcement-based intervention.

9. Combination interventions do not show an increasing trend. When they do occur, they are likely to be carried out by typical agents and in typical settings.

10. With respect to systems change, significant others are increasingly likely to alter their behavior as part of the intervention. No trend is seen, however, for environmental reorganization, a critical aspect of systems change.

11. Intervention in all relevant contexts does not show a trend. When it does occur, it is likely to be done by typical agents and in typical settings.

12. There is an increase over time in outcomes associated with short-term

maintenance (5 months or less) but none for longer-term maintenance.

13. Outcomes associated with generalization, lifestyle change, and social validity show no trends and are few in number.

How Effective is PBS?

1. Modest to substantial increases in positive behavior are typically observed following the application of PBS intervention.

2. With respect to reduction in problem behavior, about one-half (using a criterion of 90% or more decrease in problem behavior from baseline) to two-thirds (using an 80% criterion) of the outcomes are successes.

3. Typically, the success rate does not change as a function of whether stimulus-based intervention and reinforcement-based intervention are used alone or in combination with each other, nor does it change when non-PBS interventions are added.

4. With respect to maintenance effects, about two-thirds of the outcomes are successes (using a 90% reduction criterion). However, the database is small and gets smaller as the duration of follow-up is lengthened.

5. There are demonstrations of successful lifestyle change and good social validity, but these data are reported only for a very small minority of outcomes.

What Factors Modulate the Effectiveness of PBS?

1. Intervention for combinations of problem behavior produces lower success rates than interventions for single types of problem behavior.

2. The success rate (using a 90% reduction criterion) for interventions based on a prior functional assessment was almost twice that obtained when this type of assessment was not conducted.

3. The success rate (90% criterion) was greater following interventions that involved systems change (although the database for one aspect of systems change, environmental reorganization, was very small).

4. The success rate (90% criterion) associated with typical agents was higher than that obtained with atypical agents. The success rates in typical versus atypical settings were comparable.

How Responsive is the PBS Literature to the Needs of Consumers (Nonresearchers)?

1. Comprehensive lifestyle support is a major goal of families, but the database rarely addressed this issue.

2. Families are most concerned with long-term behavior change. The database, in a minority of cases, demonstrated such change. However, no outcomes involved follow-up of

longer than 2 years, which poses difficulties for the vast majority of families that think of maintenance in terms of decades, rather than months.

3. Consumers (e.g., parents, teachers) judge interventions in terms of their practicality and relevance and are concerned with how well intervention plans mesh with the realities of the complex social systems in which the consumers must function. The database, more concerned with issues of rigor and demonstrations of experimental control, generally failed to focus on larger consumer goals.

4. Consumers are concerned with obtaining support for themselves in addition to support for people with disabilities. This topic was not a focus of systematic research in the studies included in the database.

CHAPTER 6
RECOMMENDATIONS

For Researchers

The main recommendation to researchers is that we need a new applied science. For a truly applied science to develop, researchers need to address consumer needs more systematically and more frequently. A robust applied science will require changes in assessment and intervention practices, a redefinition of what constitutes a significant outcome, and measurement procedures that address these new priorities.

With respect to assessment, methods must be developed that are user-friendly, are feasible in the community, and yield accurate information. Functional analysis meets the last criterion but not the first two; it therefore needs to be supplemented and often replaced with a new generation of assessment tools that meet all three criteria and can be implemented repeatedly as circumstances warrant.

With respect to advancing intervention practices, researchers need to focus on consumer goals pertaining to comprehensive lifestyle support, long-term change, and direct support to consumers themselves. These goals can most plausibly be met by an increasing emphasis on multicomponent interventions that are linked to assessment information, broad reorganization of context (systems change), an emphasis on ecological validity (typical agents and typical settings), intervention in all relevant contexts, and the application of all these practices over protracted periods of time. The consumer goals just noted together with the goals of practicality and relevance can be best met by focusing on

how well intervention practices fit with specific contexts (goodness-of-fit), and this determination can be made through the active participation of consumers in the research process as advisers and/or collaborators (Participatory Action Research).

Finally, with respect to outcomes, the PAR model needs to be adapted as well in order to define, in specific terms, the dimensions of new outcome measures defined primarily in terms of long-term, socially validated, comprehensive lifestyle change and only secondarily in terms of reductions in problem behavior.

For Service Providers

The main recommendation to service providers is to fix problem contexts, not problem behavior. Problem contexts (i.e., environmental deficiencies and skill deficits) are the fertile ground from which problem behavior springs. Therefore, whenever problem behavior is identified as a clinical issue, service providers ought first and foremost to structure intervention so that it reflects a knowledge (derived from systematic assessment) of what is wrong with the individual's environment (e.g., educational practices, scheduling issues, lack of control) and skill repertoire (e.g., lack of communication, poorly developed social skills, insufficient self-management). Such assessment information can then be used to redesign the environment and enhance the individual's adaptive skill repertoire. The primary effect of this approach is to strengthen positive behaviors. An important but secondary effect is to produce a decrease in problem behavior.

85

Reflecting consumer needs, service providers need to offer hands-on, ongoing (rather than episodic) support to families, teachers, and staff over long periods of time. This strategy has the dual effect of supporting the consumers themselves and gradually permitting a transfer of support tactics from the professional service provider to typical intervention agents.

The PAR model for researchers is also appropriate for service providers. Specifically, service providers need to transform their role from experts who unilaterally select goals and structure interventions, to collaborators who, in consort with consumers, define the dimensions of comprehensive lifestyle change (thereby ensuring social validity) in a manner that represents a good fit with the reality of day-to-day contextual constraints (thereby ensuring practicality and relevance).

For Social Policy Advocates

The main recommendation for social policy advocates is that regulations defining quality of services need to mandate standards of best practice. These standards should involve or address:

- repeated functional assessments that identify, on an ongoing basis, the environmental and behavioral deficiencies that are the root cause of problem behavior;

- direct linkage between assessment information and the design of interventions;

- intervention in all relevant contexts, a strategy that almost invariably means the use of multicomponent interventions geared toward altering systems, not just discrete behaviors;

- ecologically valid relevant contexts (i.e., typical agents carry out intervention in typical settings);

- the long-term perspectives of consumers—by designing and redesigning interventions as changes in life circumstances warrant; that is, intervention plans must have a lifespan orientation rather than a crisis management orientation;

- consumers being an integral part of the system by constructing interventions that respond to the personal needs and concerns of consumers (goodness-of-fit) thereby ensuring practicality and relevance;

- social validity issues, defining outcome goals in terms of comprehensive lifestyle change and support and not just reduction in problem behavior.

For the Government

The main recommendation for government is that resources should be invested to ensure the continued development and evaluation of a truly applied science of PBS that is sensitive to consumer needs. Government can strengthen this process by (a) developing grant competitions that require adherence to best practices, emphasizing the demonstration of socially valid comprehensive lifestyle change rather than microanalysis of cause-and-effect processes in situations that lack ecological validity; (b) creating a nationally accessible database on PBS that is updated periodically so that consumers, advocates, policy analysts, and researchers can study the database to see what progress is being made, what the gaps are, and what future directions might be fruitful; (c) convening periodic state-of-the-art conferences that define where we are and how PBS needs to change to keep abreast of new developments in policy, advocacy, consumer needs, and research findings.

REFERENCES

References marked with an asterisk indicate studies included in the synthesis.

Albin, R. W., Lucyshyn, J. M., Horner, R. H., & Flannery, K. B. (1996). Contextual fit for behavior support plans. In L. K. Koegel, R. L. Koegel, & G. Dunlap (Eds.), *Positive behavioral support: Including people with difficult behavior in the community* (pp. 81–98). Baltimore: Paul H. Brookes.

*Albin, R. W., O'Brien, M., & Horner, R. H. (1995). Analysis of an escalating sequence of problem behaviors: A case study. *Research in Developmental Disabilities, 16,* 133–147.

Aman, M. G., Singh, N. N., Stewart, A. W., & Field, C. J. (1985). Psychometric characteristics of the Aberrant Behavior Checklist. *American Journal of Mental Deficiency, 89,* 492–502.

Arendt, R. E., MacLean, W. E., & Baumeister, A. A. (1988). Critique of sensory integration therapy and its application in mental retardation. *American Journal on Mental Retardation, 92,* 401–411.

Axelrod, S. (1987). Doing it without arrows. [Review of the book *Alternatives to punishment: Solving behavior problems with non-aversive strategies*]. *The Behavior Analyst, 10,* 243–251.

Baer, D. M., Wolf, M. M., & Risley, T. R. (1968). Some current dimensions of applied behavior analysis. *Journal of Applied Behavior Analysis, 1,* 91–97.

Bailey, J. S., & Pyles, D. A. M. (1989). Behavioral diagnostics. In E. Cipani (Ed.), *The treatment of severe behavior disorders* (Monograph No. 12, pp. 85–107). Washington, DC: American Association on Mental Retardation.

*Ballard, K. D., & Medland, J. L. (1986). Collateral effects from teaching attention, imitation, and toy interaction behaviors to a developmentally handicapped child. *Child and Family Behavior Therapy, 7*(4), 47–60.

*Bambara, L. M., Koger, F., Katzer, T., & Davenport, T. A. (1995). Embedding choice in the context of daily routines: An experimental case study. *Journal of The Association for Persons With Severe Handicaps, 20,* 185–195.

Bannerman, D. J., Sheldon, J. B., Sherman, J. A., & Harchik, A. E. (1990). Balancing the right to habilitation with the right to personal liberties: The rights of people with developmental disabilities to eat too many doughnuts and take a nap. *Journal of Applied Behavior Analysis, 23,* 79–89.

Barrett, R. P. (Ed.). (1986). *Severe behavior disorders in the mentally retarded.* New York: Plenum.

Bijou, S. W., & Baer, D. M. (1961). *Child development I: A systematic and empirical theory.* Englewood Cliffs, NJ: Prentice-Hall.

Bijou, S. W., Peterson, R. F., & Ault, M. H. (1968). A method to integrate description and experimental field studies at the level of data and empirical concepts. *Journal of Applied Behavior Analysis, 1,* 175–191.

Billingsley, B. S., & Cross, L. H. (1991). Teachers' decisions to transfer from special to general education. *Journal of Special Education, 24,* 496–511.

Billups, L. H. (1997). Response to bridging the research-to-practice gap. *Exceptional Children, 63,* 525–527.

Bird, F., Dores, P. A., Moniz, D., & Robinson, J. (1989). Reducing severe aggressive and self-injurious behaviors with functional communication training. *American Journal on Mental Retardation, 94,* 37–48.

*Blum, N. J., Mauk, J. E., McComas, J. J., & Mace, F. C. (1996). Separate and combined effects of methylphenidate and a behavioral intervention on disruptive behavior in children with mental retardation. *Journal of Applied Behavior Analysis, 29,* 305–319.

Bodfish, J. W., & Madison, J. T. (1993). Diagnosis and fluoxetine treatment of compulsive behavior disorder of adults with mental retardation. *American Journal on Mental Retardation, 98,* 360–367.

*Bowman, L. G., Fisher, W. W., Thompson, R. H., & Piazza, C. C. (1997). On the relation of mands and the function of destructive behavior. *Journal of Applied Behavior Analysis, 30,* 251–265.

Braddock, D., Hemp, R., Fujiura, G., Bachelder, L., & Mitchell, D. (1990). *The state of the states in developmental disabilities.* Baltimore: Paul H. Brookes.

Bronfenbrenner, U. (1989). Ecological systems theory. In R. Vasta (Ed.), *Annals of Child Development* (Vol. 6, pp. 187–249). Greenwich, CT: JAI Press.

Browder, D. M. (1997). Educating students with severe disabilities: Enhancing the conversation between research and practice. *The Journal of Special Education, 31,* 137–144.

Brown, F. (1991). Creative daily scheduling: A nonintrusive approach to challenging behaviors in community residences. *Journal of The Association for Persons With Severe Handicaps, 16,* 75–84.

Browning, R., & Stover, D. (1971). *Behavior modification in child treatment: An experimental and clinical approach.* Chicago: Aldine Atherton.

Bruyère, S. M. (1993). Participatory action research: Overview and implications for family members of persons with disabilities. *Journal of Vocational Rehabilitation, 3*(2), 62–68.

Bucher, B., & Lovaas, O. I. (1968). Use of aversive stimulation in behavior modification. In M. R. Jones (Ed.), *Miami symposium on the prediction of behavior, 1967: Aversive stimulation* (pp. 77–145). Coral Gables, FL: University of Miami Press.

Busk, P. L., & Serlin, R. C. (1992). Meta-analysis for single-case research. In T. Kratochwill and J. Levin (Eds.), *Single case research design and analysis: New directions for psychology and education* (pp. 187–212). Hillsdale, NJ: Lawrence Erlbaum.

Cameron, M. J., Ainsleigh, S. A., & Bird, F. L. (1992). The acquisition of stimulus control of compliance and participation during an ADL routine. *Behavioral Residential Treatment, 7,* 327–340.

*Cameron, M. J., Luiselli, J. K., McGrath, M., & Carlton, R. (1992). Stimulus control analysis and treatment of noncompliant behavior. *Journal of Developmental and Physical Disabilities, 4,* 141–150.

*Campbell, R. V., & Lutzker, J. R. (1993). Using functional equivalence training to reduce severe challenging behavior: A case study. *Journal of Developmental and Physical Disabilities, 5,* 203–216.

Carnine, D. (1997). Bridging the research-to-practice gap. *Exceptional Children, 63,* 513–521.

Carr, E. G. (1977). The motivation of self-injurious behavior: A review of some hypotheses. *Psychological Bulletin, 84,* 800–816.

Carr, E. G. (1988). Functional equivalence as a mechanism of response generalization. In R. H. Horner, R. L. Koegel, & G. Dunlap (Eds.), *Generalization and maintenance: Lifestyle changes in applied settings* (pp. 194–219). Baltimore: Paul H. Brookes.

Carr, E. G. (1993). Behavior analysis is not ultimately about behavior. *The Behavior Analyst, 16,* 47–49.

Carr, E. G. (1994). Emerging themes in the functional analysis of problem behavior. *Journal of Applied Behavior Analysis, 27,* 393–399.

*Carr, E. G., & Carlson, J. I. (1993). Reduction of severe behavior problems in the community using a multicomponent treatment approach. *Journal of Applied Behavior Analysis, 26,* 157–172.

Carr, E. G., Carlson, J. I., Langdon, N. A., Magito McLaughlin, D., & Yarbrough, S. C. (1998). Two perspectives on antecedent control: Molecular and molar. In J. K. Luiselli & M. J. Cameron (Eds.), *Antecedent control: Innovative approaches to behavioral support* (pp. 3–28). Baltimore: Paul H. Brookes.

*Carr, E. G., & Durand, V. M. (1985). Reducing behavior problems through functional communication training. *Journal of Applied Behavior Analysis, 18,* 111–126.

Carr, E. G., Levin, L., McConnachie, G., Carlson, J. I., Kemp, D. C., & Smith, C. E. (1994). *Communication-based intervention for problem behavior. A user's guide for producing positive change.* Baltimore: Paul H. Brookes.

Carr, E. G., & Lovaas, O. I. (1983). Contingent electric shock as a treatment for severe behavior problems. In S. Axelrod & J. Apsche (Eds.), *Punishment: Its effects on human behavior* (pp. 221–245). New York: Academic Press.

Carr, E. G., & McDowell, J. J. (1980). Social control of self-injurious behavior of organic etiology. *Behavior Therapy, 11,* 402–409.

*Carr, E. G., & Newsom, C. (1985). Demand-related tantrums: Conceptualization and treatment. *Behavior Modification, 9,* 403–426.

Carr, E. G., Newsom, C. D., & Binkoff, J. A. (1976). Stimulus control of self-destructive behavior in a psychotic child. *Journal of Abnormal Child Psychology, 4,* 139–153.

Carr, E. G., Newsom, C. D., & Binkoff, J. A. (1980). Escape as a factor in the aggressive behavior of two retarded children. *Journal of Applied Behavior Analysis, 13*, 101–117.

Carr, E. G., Robinson, S., Taylor, J. C., & Carlson, J. I. (1990). *Positive approaches to the treatment of severe behavior problems in persons with developmental disabilities: A review and analysis of reinforcement and stimulus-based procedures.* (Monograph No. 4). Seattle: The Association for Persons With Severe Handicaps.

Carr, E. G., & Smith, C. E. (1995). Biological setting events for self-injury. *Mental Retardation and Developmental Disabilities Research Reviews, 1,* 94–98.

Cataldo, M. F. (1991). The effects of punishment and other behavior-reducing procedures on the destructive behaviors of persons with developmental disabilities. In *Treatment of destructive behaviors in persons with developmental disabilities* (NIH Publication No. 91-2410, pp. 231–341). Washington, DC: National Institutes of Health.

*Cataldo, M. F., Ward, E. M., Russo, D. C., Riordan, M., & Bennett, D. (1986). Compliance and correlated problem behavior in children: Effects of contingent and noncontingent reinforcement. *Analysis and Intervention in Developmental Disabilities, 6,* 265–282.

*Charlop, M. H., Kurtz, P. F., & Milstein, J. P. (1992). Too much reinforcement, too little behavior: Assessing task interspersal procedures in conjunction with different reinforcement schedules with autistic children. *Journal of Applied Behavior Analysis, 25,* 795–808.

*Clarke, S., Dunlap, G., Foster-Johnson, L., Childs, K. E., Wilson, D., White, R., & Vera, A. (1995). Improving the conduct of students with behavioral disorders by incorporating student interests into curricular activities. *Behavioral Disorders, 20*(4), 221–237.

Cohen, J. (1960). A coefficient of agreement for nominal scales. *Educational and Psychological Measurement, 20,* 37–46.

*Cooper, L. J., Wacker, D. P., Thursby, D., Plagmann, L. A., Harding, J., Millard, T., & Derby, M. (1992). Analysis of the effects of task preferences, task demands, and adult attention on child behavior in outpatient and classroom settings. *Journal of Applied Behavior Analysis, 25,* 823–840.

Copeland, K. (1997). Worming our way into the system, or as the worm turns. *The Communicator, 8*(2), 20–22.

Dadson, S., & Horner, R. H. (1993). Manipulating setting events to decrease problem behaviors: A case study. *Teaching Exceptional Children, 25*(3), 53–55.

*Day, H. M., Horner, R. H., & O'Neill, R. E. (1994). Multiple functions of problem behaviors: Assessment and intervention. *Journal of Applied Behavior Analysis, 27,* 279–289.

*Day, R. M., Rea, J. A., Schussler, N. G., Larsen, S. E., & Johnson, W. L. (1988). A functionally based approach to the treatment of self-injurious behavior. *Behavior Modification, 12,* 565–589.

Dennis, R. E., Williams, W., Giangreco, M. F., & Cloninger, C. J. (1993). Quality of life as a context for planning and evaluation of services for people with disabilities. *Exceptional Children, 59,* 499–512.

Derby, K. M., Wacker, D. P., Sasso, G., Northup, J., Cigrand, K., & Asmus, J. (1992). Brief functional assessment techniques to evaluate aberrant behavior in an outpatient setting: A summary of 79 cases. *Journal of Applied Behavior Analysis, 25,* 713–721.

Desrochers, M. N., Hile, M. G., & Williams-Moseley, T. L. (1997). Survey of functional assessment procedures used with individuals who display mental retardation and severe problem behaviors. *American Journal on Mental Retardation, 101,* 535–546.

Didden, R., Duker, P. C., & Korzilius, H. (1997). Meta-analytic study on treatment effectiveness for problem behaviors with individuals who have mental retardation. *American Journal on Mental Retardation, 101,* 387–399.

Donnellan, A. M., LaVigna, G. W., Negri-Shoultz, N., & Fassbender, L. L. (1988). *Progress without punishment: Effective approaches for learners with severe behavior problems.* New York: Teachers College Press.

*Donnellan, A. M., LaVigna, G. W., Zambito, J., & Thvedt, J. (1985). A time-limited intensive intervention program model to support community placement for persons with severe behavior problems. *Journal of The Association for Persons With Severe Handicaps, 10,* 123–131.

*Ducharme, J. M., Lucas, H., & Pontes, E. (1994). Errorless embedding in the reduction of severe maladaptive behavior during interactive and learning tasks. *Behavior Therapy, 25,* 489–501.

*Ducharme, J. M., Pontes, E., Guger, S., Crozier, K., Lucas, H., & Popynick, M. (1994). Errorless compliance to parental requests II: Increasing clinical practicality through abbreviation of treatment parameters. *Behavior Therapy, 25,* 469–487.

*Ducharme, J. M., & Popynik, M. (1993). Errorless compliance to parental requests: Treatment effects and generalization. *Behavior Therapy, 24,* 209–226.

Dunlap, G., dePerczel, M., Clarke, S., Wilson, D., Wright, S., White, R., & Gomez, A. (1994). Choice making and proactive behavioral support for students with emotional and behavioral challenges. *Journal of Applied Behavior Analysis, 27,* 505–518.

*Dunlap, G., Foster-Johnson, L., Clarke, S., Kern, L., & Childs, K. E. (1995). Modifying activities to produce functional outcomes: Effects on the problem behaviors of students with disabilities. *Journal of The Association for Persons With Severe Handicaps, 20,* 248–258.

*Dunlap, G., Kern-Dunlap, L., Clarke, S., & Robbins, F. R. (1991). Functional assessment, curricular revision, and severe problems. *Journal of Applied Behavior Analysis, 24,* 387–397.

Dunlap, G., & Koegel, R. L. (1980). Motivating autistic children through stimulus variation. *Journal of Applied Behavior Analysis, 13,* 619–627.

Dunlap, G., & Robbins, F. R. (1991). Current perspectives in service delivery for young children with autism. *Comprehensive Mental Health Care, 1,* 177–189.

Dunlap, G., Robbins, F. R., & Darrow, M. A. (1994). Parents' reports of their children's challenging behaviors: Results of a statewide survey. *Mental Retardation, 32,* 206–212.

Dunst, C. J., Trivette, C. M., & Jodry, W. (1997). Influences of social support on children with disabilities and their families. In M. J. Guralnick (Ed.), *The effectiveness of early intervention* (pp. 499–522). Baltimore: Paul H. Brookes.

Durand, V. M. (1990). *Functional communication training: An intervention program for severe behavior problems.* New York: Guilford.

*Durand, V. M. (1993). Functional communication training using assistive devices: Effects on challenging behavior and affect. *Augmentative and Alternative Communication, 9,* 168–176.

*Durand, V. M., & Carr, E. G. (1991). Functional communication training to reduce challenging behavior: Maintenance and application in new settings. *Journal of Applied Behavior Analysis, 24,* 251–264.

*Durand, V. M., & Carr, E. G. (1992). An analysis of maintenance following functional communication training. *Journal of Applied Behavior Analysis, 25,* 777–794.

Durand, V. M., & Crimmins, D. B. (1988). Identifying the variables maintaining self-injurious behavior. *Journal of Autism and Developmental Disorders, 18,* 99–117.

Durand, V. M., & Crimmins, D. B. (1992). *The motivation assessment scale (MAS) administration guide.* Topeka, KS: Monaco & Associates.

*Durand, V. M., & Kishi, G. (1987). Reducing severe behavior problems among persons with dual sensory impairments: An evaluation of a technical assistance model. *Journal of The Association for Persons With Severe Handicaps, 12,* 2–10.

*Dyer, K., Dunlap, G., & Winterling, V. (1990). Effects of choice making on the serious problem behaviors of students with severe handicaps. *Journal of Applied Behavior Analysis, 23,* 515–524.

*Egan, P. J., Zlomke, L. C., & Bush, B. R. (1993). Utilizing functional assessment, behavioral consultation and videotape review of treatment to reduce aggression: A case study. *Special Services in the Schools, 7,* 27–37.

Emerson, E., McGill, P., & Mansell, J. (Eds.). (1994). *Severe learning disabilities and challenging behaviours.* London: Chapman & Hall.

Evans, I. M., & Meyer, L. H. (1985). *An educative approach to behavior problems: A practical decision model for interventions with severely handicapped learners.* Baltimore: Paul H. Brookes.

Evans, I. M., & Scotti, J. R. (1989). Defining meaningful outcomes for persons with profound disabilities. In F. Brown & D. Lehr (Eds.), *Persons with profound disabilities: Issues and practices* (pp. 83–107). Baltimore: Paul H. Brookes.

The Family Connection staff, DeVault, G., Krug, C., & Fake, S. (1996). Why does Samantha act that way? *Exceptional Parent, 26*(9), 43–47.

Favell, J. E., McGimsey, J. F., & Schell, R. M. (1982). Treatment of self-injury by providing alternate sensory activities. *Analysis and Intervention in Developmental Disabilities, 2,* 83–104.

Feldman, M. A. (1990). Balancing freedom from harm and right to treatment for persons with developmental disabilities. In A. C. Repp & N. N. Singh (Eds.), *Perspectives on the use of nonaversive and aversive interventions for persons with developmental disabilities* (pp. 261–271). Sycamore, IL: Sycamore.

Fimian, M. J. (1986). Social support and occupational stress in special education. *Exceptional Children, 52,* 436–442.

*Fisher, W. W., Piazza, C. C., Bowman, L. G., Hanley, G. P., & Adelinis, J. D. (1997). Direct and collateral effects of restraints and restraint fading. *Journal of Applied Behavior Analysis, 30,* 105–119.

*Fisher, W. W., Piazza, C. C., Cataldo, M. F., Harrell, R., Jefferson, G., & Conner, R. (1993). Functional communication training with and without extinction and punishment. *Journal of Applied Behavior Analysis, 26,* 23–36.

*Fisher, W. W., Piazza, C. C., & Page, T. J. (1989). Assessing independent and interactive effects of behavioral and pharmacologic interventions for a client with dual diagnoses. *Journal of Behavior Therapy and Experimental Psychiatry, 20,* 241–250.

*Flannery, K. B., & Horner, R. H. (1994). The relationship between predictability and problem behavior for students with severe disabilities. *Journal of Behavioral Education, 4,* 157–176.

Foxx, R. M. (1982). *Decreasing behaviors of severely retarded and autistic persons.* Champaign, IL: Research Press.

Foxx, R. M. (1990). "Harry": A ten year follow-up of the successful treatment of a self-injurious man. *Research in Developmental Disabilities, 11,* 67–76.

Foxx, R. M., Bittle, R. G., & Faw, G. D. (1989). A maintenance strategy for discontinuing aversive procedures: A 52-month follow-up of the treatment of aggression. *American Journal on Mental Retardation, 94,* 27–36.

*Friman, P. C., Barnard, J. D., Altman, K., & Wolf, M. M. (1986). Parent and teacher use of DRO and DRI to reduce aggressive behavior. *Analysis and Intervention in Developmental Disabilities, 6,* 319–330.

Fuchs, D., & Fuchs, L. S. (1990). Making educational research more important. *Exceptional Children, 57,* 102–107.

Gardner, W. I., Cole, C. L., Berry, D. L., & Nowinski, J. M. (1983). Reduction of disruptive behaviors in mentally retarded adults: A self-management approach. *Behavior Modification, 7,* 76–96.

Gardner, W. I., & Sovner, R. (1994). *Self-injurious behavior.* Willow Street, PA: VIDA.

Gardner, W. I., & Whalen, J. P. (1996). Discussion: A multimodal behavior analytic model for evaluating the effects of medical problems on nonspecific behavioral symptoms in persons with developmental disabilities. *Behavioral Interventions, 11,* 147–161.

Gersten, R., & Brengelman, S. U. (1996). The quest to translate research into classroom practice. *Remedial and Special Education, 17,* 67–74.

Gersten, R., Morvant, M., & Brengelman, S. (1995). Close to the classroom is close to the bone: Coaching as a means to translate research into classroom practice. *Exceptional Children, 62,* 52–66.

*Grace, N., Cowart, C., & Matson, J. L. (1988). Reinforcement and self-control for treating a chronic case of self-injury in Lesch-Nyhan syndrome. *Journal of the Multihandicapped Person, 1,* 53–59.

Green, G., & Shane, H. C. (1994). Science, reason, and facilitated communication. *Journal of The Association for Persons With Severe Handicaps, 19,* 151–172.

Guess, D., Helmstetter, E., Turnbull, H. R. III, & Knowlton, S. (1987). *Use of aversive procedures with persons who are disabled: An historical review and critical analysis.* (Monograph No. 2). Seattle: The Association for Persons With Severe Handicaps.

Guess, D., & Siegel-Causey, D. (1995). Attractor dimensions of behavior state changes among individuals with profound disabilities. *American Journal on Mental Retardation, 99,* 642–663.

Hall R. V., Lund, D., & Jackson, D. (1968). Effects of teacher attention on study behavior. *Journal of Applied Behavior Analysis, 1,* 1–12.

*Hanley, G. P., Piazza, C. C., & Fisher, W. W. (1997). Noncontingent presentation of attention and substitute stimuli in the treatment of attention-maintained destructive behavior. *Journal of Applied Behavior Analysis, 30,* 229–237.

Haring, T. G. (1996). The role of research in the continuing development of the field of severe disabilities. *Journal of The Association for Persons With Severe Handicaps, 21,* 6–8.

Haring, T. G., & Kennedy, C. H. (1990). Contextual control of problem behavior in students with severe disabilities. *Journal of Applied Behavior Analysis, 23,* 235–243.

Harris, S. L., & Ersner-Hershfield, R. (1978). Behavioral suppression of seriously disruptive behavior in psychotic and retarded patients: A review of punishment and its alternatives. *Psychological Bulletin, 85,* 1352–1375.

Harry, B., Allen, N., & McLaughlin, M. (1995). Communication versus compliance: African-American parents' involvement in special education. *Exceptional Children, 61,* 364–377.

Harry, B., Grenot-Scheyer, M., Smith-Lewis, M., Park, H-S., Xin, F., & Schwartz, I. (1995). Developing culturally inclusive services for individuals with severe disabilities. *Journal of The Association for Persons With Severe Handicaps, 20,* 99–109.

Hays, C. D. (1997). A new perspective. *The Positive Behavior Support Newsletter, 1*(3), 2–3.

Hersen, M., & Barlow, D. H. (1976). *Single case experimental designs.* New York: Pergamon.

Hess, P. M., & Mullen, E. J. (Eds). (1995). *Practitioner-research partnership: Building knowledge from, in, and for practice.* Annapolis, MD: NASW Press.

Horner, R. (1980). The effects of an environmental "enrichment" program on the behavior of institutionalized profoundly retarded children. *Journal of Applied Behavior Analysis, 13,* 473–491.

*Horner, R. H., & Budd, C. M. (1985). Acquisition of manual sign use: Collateral reduction of maladaptive behavior, and factors limiting generalization. *Education and Training of the Mentally Retarded, 20,* 39–47.

Horner, R. H., Close, D. W., Fredericks, H. D. B., O'Neill, R. E., Albin, R. W., Sprague, J. R., Kennedy, C. H., Flannery, K. B., & Heathfield, L. T. (1996). Supported living for people with profound disabilities and severe problem behaviors. In D. H. Lehr & F. Brown (Eds.), *People with disabilities who challenge the system* (pp. 209–240). Baltimore: Paul H. Brookes.

*Horner, R. H., & Day, H. M. (1991). The effects of response efficiency on functionally equivalent competing behaviors. *Journal of Applied Behavior Analysis, 24,* 719–732.

*Horner, R. H., Day, H. M., & Day, J. R. (1997). Using neutralizing routines to reduce problem behaviors. *Journal of Applied Behavior Analysis, 30,* 601–614.

*Horner, R. H., Day, H. M., Sprague, J. R., O'Brien, M., & Heathfield, L. T. (1991). Interspersed requests: A nonaversive procedure for reducing aggression and self-injury during instruction. *Journal of Applied Behavior Analysis, 24,* 265–278.

Horner, R. H., Diemer, S., & Brazeau, K. (1992). Educational support for students with severe problem behaviors in Oregon: A descriptive analysis from the 1987–1988 school year. *Journal of The Association for Persons With Severe Handicaps, 17,* 154–169.

Horner, R. H., Dunlap, G., & Koegel, R. L. (Eds.). (1988). *Generalization and maintenance in applied settings.* Baltimore: Paul H. Brookes.

Horner, R. H., Dunlap, G., Koegel, R. L., Carr, E. G., Sailor, W., Anderson, J., Albin, R. W., & O'Neill, R. E. (1990). Toward a technology of "nonaversive" behavioral support. *Journal of The Association for Persons With Severe Handicaps, 15,* 125–132.

*Horner, R. H., Sprague, J. R., O'Brien, M., & Heathfield, L. T. (1990). The role of response efficiency in the reduction of problem behaviors through functional equivalence training: A case study. *Journal of The Association for Persons With Severe Handicaps, 15,* 91–97.

95

Horner, R. H., Vaughn, B. J., Day, H. M., & Ard, W. R. (1996). The relationship between setting events and problem behavior: Expanding our understanding of behavioral support. In L. K. Koegel, R. L. Koegel, & G. Dunlap (Eds.), *Positive behavioral support: Including people with difficult behavior in the community* (pp. 381–402). Baltimore: Paul H. Brookes.

Hoshmand, L. T., & Polkinghorne, D. E. (1992). Redefining the science-practice relationship and professional training. *American Psychologist, 47,* 55–66.

Huberman, M. (1990). Linkage between researchers and practitioners: A qualitative study. *American Educational Research Journal, 27,* 363–391.

Hughes, C., Hwang, B., Kim, J. H., Eisenman, L. T., & Killian, D. J. (1995). Quality of life in applied research: A review and analysis of empirical measures. *American Journal on Mental Retardation, 99,* 623–641.

*Hunt, P., Alwell, M., Goetz, L., & Sailor, W. (1990). Generalized effects of conversation skill training. *Journal of The Association for Persons With Severe Handicaps, 15,* 250–260.

Individuals With Disabilities Education Act., Pub. L. No. 105-117, 20 U.S.C. § 1401 *et seq.* (1997).

Iwata, B. A., Dorsey, M. F., Slifer, K. J., Bauman, K. E., & Richman, G. S. (1982). Toward a functional analysis of self-injury. *Analysis and Intervention in Developmental Disabilities, 2,* 3–20.

*Iwata, B. A., Pace, G. M., Kalsher, M. J., Cowdery, G. E., & Cataldo, M. F. (1990). Experimental analysis and extinction of self-injurious escape behavior. *Journal of Applied Behavior Analysis, 23,* 11–27.

*Iwata, B. A., Pace, G. M., Willis, K. D., Gamache, T. B., & Hyman, S. L. (1986). Operant studies of self-injurious hand biting in the Rett's syndrome. *American Journal of Medical Genetics* (Suppl. 1), 157–166.

*Jansma, P., & Combs, C. S. (1987). The effects of fitness training and reinforcement on maladaptive behaviors of institutionalized adults, classified as mentally retarded/emotionally disturbed. *Education and Training in Mental Retardation, 22,* 268–279.

*Jayne, D., Schloss, P. J., Alper, S., & Menscher, S. (1994). Reducing disruptive behaviors by training students to request assistance. *Behavior Modification, 18,* 320–338.

*Jones, D. B., & Van Houten, R. (1985). The use of daily quizzes and public posting to decrease disruptive behavior of secondary school students. *Education and Treatment of Children, 8,* 91–106.

Jones, S. (1997, May). The Friendly Connection works at E. C. Glass. *Positive Behavior Support Times, 1*(1), 1.

*Karsh, K. G., Repp, A. C., Dahlquist, C. M., & Munk, D. (1995). In vivo functional assessment and multi-element interventions for problem behaviors of students with disabilities in classroom settings. *Journal of Behavioral Education, 5,* 189–210.

Kaufman, M., Schiller, E., Birman, B., & Coutinho, M. (1993). A federal perspective on improving practices, programs, and policies in special education. *Evaluation and Program Planning, 16,* 263–269.

Kazdin, A. E. (1980). *Behavior modification in applied settings* (Rev. ed.). Homewood, IL: Dorsey Press.

*Kehle, T. J., Clark, E., Jenson, W. R., & Wampold, B. E. (1986). Effectiveness of self-observation with behavior disordered elementary school children. *School Psychology Review, 15,* 289–295.

*Kemp, D. C., & Carr, E. G. (1995). Reduction of severe problem behavior in community employment using an hypothesis-driven multicomponent intervention approach. *Journal of The Association for Persons With Severe Handicaps, 20,* 229–247.

*Kennedy, C. H. (1994). Manipulating antecedent conditions to alter the stimulus control of problem behavior. *Journal of Applied Behavior Analysis, 27,* 161–170.

*Kennedy, C. H., & Haring, T. G. (1993). Combining reward and escape DRO to reduce the problem behavior of students with severe disabilities. *Journal of The Association for Persons With Severe Handicaps, 18,* 85–92.

*Kennedy, C. H., & Itkonen, T. (1993). Effects of setting events on the problem behavior of students with severe disabilities. *Journal of Applied Behavior Analysis, 26,* 321–327.

*Kennedy, C. H., & Souza, G. (1995). Functional analysis and treatment of eye poking. *Journal of Applied Behavior Analysis, 28,* 27–37.

Kincaid, D. K. (1992, March). *Positive behavior support training.* Morgantown, WV: University Affiliated Center for Developmental Disabilities (Shawnee Hills Community Mental/Health Retardation Center).

Kincaid, D. (1996). Person-centered planning. In L. K. Koegel, R. L. Koegel, & G. Dunlap (Eds.), *Positive behavioral support: Including people with difficult behavior in the community* (pp. 439–466). Baltimore: Paul H. Brookes.

*Knapczyk, D. R. (1988). Reducing aggressive behaviors in special and regular class settings by training alternative social responses. *Behavioral Disorders, 14,* 27–39.

*Koegel, R. L., Dyer, K., & Bell, L. K. (1987). The influence of child-preferred activities on autistic children's social behavior. *Journal of Applied Behavior Analysis, 20,* 243–252.

Koegel, L. K., Koegel, R. L., & Dunlap, G. (Eds.). (1996). *Positive behavioral support: Including people with difficult behavior in the community.* Baltimore: Paul H. Brookes.

*Koegel, L. K., Koegel, R. L., Hurley, C., & Frea, W. D. (1992). Improving social skills and disruptive behavior in children with autism through self-management. *Journal of Applied Behavior Analysis, 25,* 341–353.

*Koegel, R. L., Koegel, L. K., & Suratt, A. (1992). Language intervention and disruptive behavior in preschool children with autism. *Journal of Autism and Developmental Disorders, 22,* 141–153.

*Konarski, E. A., & Johnson, M. R. (1989). The use of brief restraint plus reinforcement to treat self-injurious behavior. *Behavioral Residential Treatment, 4,* 45–52.

*Lalli, J. S., Browder, D. M., Mace, F. C., & Brown, D. K. (1993). Teacher use of descriptive analysis data to implement interventions to decrease students' problem behaviors. *Journal of Applied Behavior Analysis, 26,* 227–238.

*Lalli, J. S., & Casey, S. D. (1996). Treatment of multiply controlled problem behavior. *Journal of Applied Behavior Analysis, 29,* 391–395.

*Lalli, J. S., Casey, S., & Kates, K. (1995). Reducing escape behavior and increasing task completion with functional communication training, extinction, and response chaining. *Journal of Applied Behavior Analysis, 28,* 261–268.

*Lam, A. L., Cole, C. L., Shapiro, E. S., & Bambara, L. M. (1994). Relative effects of self-monitoring on-task behavior, academic accuracy, and disruptive behavior in students with behavior disorders. *School Psychology Review, 23,* 44–58.

Lancioni, G. E., & Hoogeveen, F. R. (1990). Non-aversive and mildly aversive procedures for reducing problem behaviours in people with developmental disorders. *Mental Handicaps Research, 3,* 137–160.

Landis, J. R., & Koch, G. G. (1977). The measurement of observer agreement for categorical data. *Biometrics, 33,* 159–174.

*Larson, J. L., & Miltenberger, R. G. (1992). The influence of antecedent exercise on problem behaviors in persons with mental retardation: A failure to replicate. *Journal of The Association for Persons With Severe Handicaps, 17,* 40–46.

Lather, P. (1986). Research as praxis. *Harvard Educational Review, 56,* 257–277.

LaVigna, G. W., & Donnellan, A. M. (1986). *Alternatives to punishment: Solving behavior problems with non-aversive strategies.* New York: Irvington.

Lee, V. L. (1988). *Beyond behaviorism.* Hillsdale, NJ: Lawrence Erlbaum.

Lennox, D. B., & Miltenberger, R. G. (1989). Conducting a functional assessment of problem behavior in applied settings. *Journal of The Association for Persons With Severe Handicaps, 14,* 304–311.

Lennox, D. B., Miltenberger, R. G., Spengler, P., & Erfanian, N. (1988). Decelerative treatment practices with persons who have mental retardation: A review of five years of the literature. *American Journal on Mental Retardation, 92,* 492–501.

*Lerman, D. C., Iwata, B. A., Smith, R. G., & Vollmer, T. R. (1994). Restraint fading and the development of alternative behavior in the treatment of self-restraint and self-injury. *Journal of Intellectual Disability Research, 38,* 135–148.

Littrell, P. C., Billingsley, B. S., & Cross, L. H. (1994). The effects of principal support on special and general educators' stress, job satisfaction, school commitment, health, and intent to stay in teaching. *Remedial and Special Education, 15,* 297–310.

Lloyd, J. W., Weintraub, F. J., & Safer, N. D. (1997). A bridge between research and practice: Building consensus. *Exceptional Children, 63,* 535–538.

Lovaas, O. I., Freitag, G., Gold, V. J., & Kassorla, I. C. (1965). Experimental studies in childhood schizophrenia: Analysis of self-destructive behavior. *Journal of Experimental Child Psychology, 2,* 67–84.

Lowry, M. A., & Sovner, R. (1992). Severe behavior problems associated with rapid cycling bipolar disorder in two adults with profound mental retardation. *Journal of Intellectual Disability Research, 36,* 269–281.

Lucyshyn, J. M., & Albin, R. W. (1993). Comprehensive support to families of children with disabilities and behavior problems: Keeping it "friendly." In G. H. S. Singer & L. E. Powers (Eds.), *Families, disability, and empowerment* (pp. 365–407). Baltimore: Paul H. Brookes.

*Lucyshyn, J. M., Albin, R. W., & Nixon, C. D. (1997). Embedding comprehensive behavioral support in family ecology: An experimental, single case analysis. *Journal of Consulting and Clinical Psychology, 65,* 241–251.

Lucyshyn, J. M., Olson, D., & Horner, R. H. (1995). Building an ecology of support: A case study of one woman with severe problem behaviors living in the community. *Journal of The Association for Persons With Severe Handicaps, 20,* 16–30.

Luiselli, J. K., & Cameron, M. J. (Eds.). (1998). *Antecedent control procedures for the behavioral support of persons with developmental disabilities.* Baltimore: Paul H. Brookes.

Lutzker, J. R., & Campbell, R. (1994). *Ecobehavioral family interventions in developmental disabilities.* Pacific Grove, CA: Brooks/Cole.

Mace, F. C. (1994). The significance and future of functional analysis methodologies. *Journal of Applied Behavior Analysis, 27,* 393–400.

*Mace, F. C., & Belfiore, P. (1990). Behavioral momentum in the treatment of escape-motivated stereotypy. *Journal of Applied Behavior Analysis, 23,* 507–514.

*Mace, F. C., Browder, D. M., & Lin, Y. (1987). Analysis of demand conditions associated with stereotypy. *Journal of Behavior Therapy and Experimental Psychiatry, 18,* 25–31.

*Mace, F. C., Browder, D. M., & Martin, D. K. (1988). Reduction of stereotypy via instruction of alternative leisure behavior. *School Psychology Review, 17,* 156–165.

Mace, F. C., Hock, M. L., Lalli, J. S., West, B. J., Belfiore, P., Pinter, E., & Brown, D. K. (1988). Behavioral momentum in the treatment of noncompliance. *Journal of Applied Behavior Analysis, 21,* 123–141.

*Maguire, K. B., Lange, B., Scherling, M., & Grow, R. (1996). The use of rehearsal and positive reinforcement in the dental treatment of uncooperative patients with mental retardation. *Journal of Developmental and Physical Disabilities, 8,* 167–177.

Malette, P., Mirenda, P., Kandborg, T., Jones, P., Bunz, T., & Rogow, S. (1992). Application of a lifestyle development process for persons with severe intellectual disabilities: A case study report. *Journal of The Association for Persons With Severe Handicaps, 17,* 179–191.

Malouf, D. B., & Schiller, E. P. (1995). Practice and research in special education. *Exceptional Children, 61,* 414–424.

*Marcus, B. A., & Vollmer, T. R. (1996). Combining noncontingent reinforcement and differential reinforcement schedules as treatment for aberrant behavior. *Journal of Applied Behavior Analysis, 29,* 43–51.

Martin, P. L., & Foxx, R. M. (1973). Victim control of the aggression of an institutionalized retardate. *Journal of Behavior Therapy and Experimental Psychiatry, 4,* 161–165.

*Mason, S. A., & Iwata, B. A. (1990). Artifactual effects of sensory-integrative therapy on self-injurious behavior. *Journal of Applied Behavior Analysis, 23,* 361–370.

*Mason, S. A., McGee, G. G., Farmer-Dougan, V., & Risley, T. R. (1989). A practical strategy for ongoing reinforcer assessment. *Journal of Applied Behavior Analysis, 22,* 171–179.

Matson, J. L., & DiLorenzo, T. M. (1984). *Punishment and its alternatives: A new perspective for behavior modification.* New York: Springer.

*Matson, J. L., & Keyes, J. (1988). Contingent reinforcement and contingent restraint to treat severe aggression and self-injury in mentally retarded adults. *Journal of the Multihandicapped Person, 1,* 141–153.

Matson, J. L., & Taras, M. E. (1989). A 20-year review of punishment and alternative methods to treat problem behaviors in developmentally delayed persons. *Research in Developmental Disabilities, 10,* 85–104.

McDowell, J. J. (1982). The importance of Herrnstein's mathematical statement of the law of effect for behavior therapy. *American Psychologist, 37,* 771–779.

Metlen, G., Majure, A., & Stroll-Reisler, C. (1996, July). A person-centered approach to supporting people with severe reputations. *TASH (The Association for Persons With Severe Handicaps) Newsletter, 22,* 7–9.

Metz, C. D. (1992a). *Life quilters: Crafty cooperation.* (Available from the Life Quilters Project, University Affiliated Center for Developmental Disabilities, 918 Chestnut Ridge Road, Suite 2, Morgantown, WV 26502)

Metz, C. D. (1992b). *Life quilters: Othello unlimited.* (Available from the Life Quilters Project, University Affiliated Center for Developmental Disabilities, 918 Chestnut Ridge Road, Suite 2, Morgantown, WV 26502)

Metz, C. D. (1992c). *Life quilters: Recycling independence project.* (Available from the Life Quilters Project, University Affiliated Center for Developmental Disabilities, 918 Chestnut Ridge Road, Suite 2, Morgantown, WV 26502)

Meyer, L. H., & Evans, I. M. (1989). *Nonaversive intervention for behavior problems.* Baltimore: Paul H. Brookes.

Meyer, L. H., & Evans, I. M. (1993). Science and practice in behavioral intervention: Meaningful outcomes, research validity, and usable knowledge. *Journal of The Association for Persons With Severe Handicaps, 18,* 224–234.

Meyer, L. H., Peck, C. A., & Brown, L. (Eds.). (1991). *Critical issues in the lives of people with severe disabilities.* Baltimore: Paul H. Brookes.

Michael, J. (1982). Distinguishing between discriminative and motivational functions of stimuli. *Journal of the Experimental Analysis of Behavior, 37,* 149–155.

*Montgomery, R. W. (1993). The collateral effect of compliance training on aggression. *Behavioral Residential Treatment, 8,* 9–20.

Morrissey, P. A. (1997). Response to bridging the research-to-practice gap. *Exceptional Children, 63,* 531–532.

Mulick, J. A., & Kedesdy, J. H. (1988). Self-injurious behavior, its treatment, and normalization. *Mental Retardation, 26,* 223–229.

Mulick, J. A., & Linscheid, T. R. (1988). [Review of the book *Alternatives to punishment: Solving behavior problems with non-aversive strategies*]. *Research in Developmental Disabilities, 9,* 317–321.

National Institutes of Health. (1991). *Treatment of destructive behaviors in persons with developmental disabilities* (NIH Publication No. 91-2410). Washington, DC: Author.

*Neufeld, A., & Fantuzzo, J. W. (1987). Treatment of severe self-injurious behavior by the mentally retarded using the bubble helmet and differential reinforcement procedures. *Journal of Behavior Therapy and Experimental Psychiatry, 18,* 127–136.

Nickels, C. (1996). A gift from Alex—The art of belonging: Strategies for academic and social inclusion. In L. K. Koegel, R. L. Koegel, & G. Dunlap (Eds.), *Positive behavioral support: Including people with difficult behavior in the community* (pp. 123–144). Baltimore: Paul H. Brookes.

Nietupski, J., Hamre-Nietupski, S., Curtin, S., & Shrikanth, K. (1997). A review of curricular research in severe disabilities from 1976 to 1995 in six selected journals. *The Journal of Special Education, 31,* 36–55.

Northup, J., Wacker, D. P., Berg, W. K., Kelly, L., Sasso, G., & DeRaad, A. (1994). The treatment of severe behavior problems in school settings using a technical assistance model. *Journal of Applied Behavior Analysis, 27,* 33–47.

O'Brien, S., & Repp, A. C. (1990). Reinforcement-based reductive procedures: A review of 20 years of their use with persons with severe or profound retardation. *Journal of The Association for Persons With Severe Handicaps, 15,* 148–159.

O'Neill, R. E., Horner, R. H., Albin, R. W., Storey, K., & Sprague, J. R. (1997a). *Functional assessment and program development for problem behavior.* Pacific Grove, CA: Brooks/Cole.

O'Neill, R. E., Horner, R. H., Albin, R. W., Storey, K., & Sprague, J. R. (1997b). *Functional analysis of problem behavior: A practical assessment guide.* Sycamore, IL: Sycamore.

*Pace, G. M., Iwata, B. A., Cowdery, G. E., Andree, P. J., & McIntyre, T. (1993). Stimulus (instructional) fading during extinction of self-injurious escape behavior. *Journal of Applied Behavior Analysis, 26,* 205–212.

*Pace, G. M., Iwata, B. A., Edwards, G. L., & McCosh, K. C. (1986). Stimulus fading and transfer in the treatment of self-restraint and self-injurious behavior. *Journal of Applied Behavior Analysis, 19,* 381–389.

Paisey, T. J. H., Whitney, R. B., & Hislop, P. M. (1990). Client characteristics and treatment selection: Legitimate influences and misleading influences. In A. C. Repp & N. N. Singh (Eds.), *Perspectives on the use of nonaversive and aversive interventions for persons with developmental disabilities* (pp. 175–197). Sycamore, IL: Sycamore.

*Paisey, T. J., Whitney, R. B., & Moore, J. (1989). Person-treatment interactions across nonaversive response-deceleration procedures for self-injury: A case study of effects and side effects. *Behavioral Residential Treatment, 4,* 69–88.

Patterson, G. R. (1982). *Coercive family process.* Eugene, OR: Castalia.

Pearman, E. L., Huang, A. M., & Mellblom, C. I. (1997). The inclusion of all students: Concerns and incentives of educators. *Education and Training in Mental Retardation and Developmental Disabilities, 32,* 11–20.

Poling, A., & Ryan, C. (1982). Differential reinforcement of other behavior schedules: Therapeutic applications. *Behavior Modifications, 6,* 3–21.

Prosser, G. (1988). Vibratory reinforcement in the field of mental handicap: A review. *Mental Handicap Research, 1,* 152–166.

Ratey, J. J., Sovner, R., Parks, A., & Rogentine, K. (1991). Busiprone treatment of aggression and anxiety in mentally retarded patients: A multiple-baseline, placebo lead-in study. *Journal of Clinical Psychiatry, 52,* 159–162.

*Realon, R. E., Favell, J. E., & Cacace, S. (1995). An economical, humane, and effective method for short-term suppression of hand mouthing. *Behavioral Interventions, 10,* 141–147.

Reichle, J. (1997). Communication intervention with persons who have severe disabilities. *The Journal of Special Education, 31,* 110–134.

Reichle, J., & Wacker, D. P. (1993). *Communicative alternatives to challenging behavior.* Baltimore: Paul H. Brookes.

Reiss, S., & Aman, M. G. (Eds.). (1998). *Psychotropic medications and developmental disabilities: The international consensus handbook.* Columbus, OH: The Ohio State University Press.

Reiss, S., & Havercamp, S. M. (1997). Sensitivity theory and mental retardation: Why functional analysis is not enough. *American Journal on Mental Retardation, 101,* 553–566.

Reiss, S., & Rojahn, J. (1993). Joint occurrence of depression and aggression in children and adults with mental retardation. *American Journal on Mental Retardation, 37,* 287–294.

*Repp, A. C., & Karsh, K. G. (1994). Hypothesis-based interventions for tantrum behaviors of persons with developmental disabilities in school settings. *Journal of Applied Behavior Analysis, 27*, 21–31.

Repp, A. C., & Singh, N. N. (Eds.). (1990). *Perspectives on the use of nonaversive and aversive interventions for persons with developmental disabilities.* Sycamore, IL: Sycamore.

Rincover, A., Cook, R., Peoples, A., & Packard, D. (1979). Sensory extinction and sensory reinforcement principles for programming multiple adaptive behavior change. *Journal of Applied Behavior Analysis, 12*, 221–233.

Risley, T. (1996). Get a life! In L. K. Koegel, R. L. Koegel, & G. Dunlap (Eds.), *Positive behavioral support: Including people with difficult behavior in the community* (pp. 425–437). Baltimore: Paul H. Brookes.

*Roberts, M. L., Mace, F. C., & Daggett, J. A. (1995). Preliminary comparisons of two negative reinforcement schedules to reduce self-injury. *Journal of Applied Behavior Analysis, 28*, 579–580.

Rolider, A., & Van Houten, R. (1990). The role of reinforcement in reducing inappropriate behavior: Some myths and misconceptions. In A. C. Repp & N. N. Singh (Eds.), *Perspectives on the use of nonaversive and aversive interventions for persons with developmental disabilities* (pp. 119–127). Sycamore, IL: Sycamore.

Ruef, M. B. (1997). *The perspectives of six stakeholder groups on the challenging behavior of individuals with mental retardation and/or autism.* Unpublished doctoral dissertation, University of Kansas, Lawrence.

S. Rep. No. 102-357, 102d Cong., 2nd Sess. 3712 et seq. (1992).

Sailor, W. (1996). New structures and systems change for comprehensive positive behavioral support. In L. K. Koegel, R. L. Koegel, & G. Dunlap (Eds.), *Positive behavioral support: Including people with difficult behavior in the community* (pp. 163–206). Baltimore: Paul H. Brookes.

*Sanders, M. R., & Plant, K. (1989). Programming for generalization to high and low risk parenting situations in families with oppositional developmentally disabled preschoolers. *Behavior Modification, 13*, 283–305.

Sands, D. J., Kozleski, E. B., & Goodwin, L. D. (1991). Whose needs are we meeting? Results of a consumer satisfaction survey of persons with developmental disabilities in Colorado. *Research in Developmental Disabilities, 12*, 297–314.

*Santarcangelo, S., Dyer, K., & Luce, S. C. (1987). Generalized reduction of disruptive behavior in unsupervised settings through specific toy training. *Journal of The Association for Persons With Severe Handicaps, 12*, 38–44.

Santelli, B., Turnbull, A. P., Marquis, J. G., & Lerner, E. P. (1993). Parent to Parent programs: Ongoing support for parents of young adults with special needs. *Journal of Vocational Rehabilitation, 3*, 25–37.

Santelli, B., Turnbull, A. P., Marquis, J. G., & Lerner, E. P. (1995). Parent to Parent programs: A unique form of mutual support. *Infants and Young Children, 8,* 48–57.

*Sasso, G. M., Reimers, T. M., Cooper, L. J., Wacker, D., Berg, W., Steege, M., Kelly, L., & Allaire, A. (1992). Use of descriptive and experimental analyses to identify the functional properties of aberrant behavior in school settings. *Journal of Applied Behavior Analysis, 25,* 809–821.

*Saunders, R. R., Saunders, M. D., Brewer, A., & Roach, T. (1996). The reduction of self-injury in two adolescents with profound retardation by the establishment of a supported routine. *Behavioral Interventions, 11,* 59–86.

Schaal, D. W., & Hackenberg, T. (1994). Toward a functional analysis of drug treatment for behavior problems of people with developmental disabilities. *American Journal on Mental Retardation, 99,* 123–140.

Schalock, R. L. (Ed.). (1996). *Quality of life: Perspectives and issues.* Washington, DC: American Association on Mental Retardation.

Schalock, R. L. (Ed.). (1990). *Quality of life: Vol. 1. Conceptualization and measurement.* Washington, DC: American Association on Mental Retardation.

Scheerenberger, R. (1990). *Public residential services for the mentally retarded: FY 1988–1990.* Fairfax, VA: National Association of Superintendents of Public Residential Facilities for the Mentally Retarded.

*Schloss, P. J., Smith, M., Santora, C., & Bryant, R. (1989). A respondent conditioning approach to reducing anger responses of a dually diagnosed man with mild mental retardation. *Behavior Therapy, 20,* 459–464.

Schroeder, S. R., & Tessel, R. (1994). Dopaminergic and serotonergic mechanisms in self-injury and aggression. In T. Thompson & D. Gray (Eds.), *Treatment of destructive behavior in developmental disabilities* (pp. 198–212). Newbury Park, CA: Sage.

Scotti, J. R., Evans, I. M., Meyer, L. H., & Walker, P. (1991). A meta-analysis of intervention research with problem behavior: Treatment validity and standards of practice. *American Journal on Mental Retardation, 96,* 233–256.

Scotti, J. R., Ujcich, K. J., Weigle, K. L., Holland, C. M., & Kirk, K. S. (1996). Interventions with challenging behavior of persons with developmental disabilities: A review of current research practices. *Journal of The Association for Persons With Severe Handicaps, 21,* 123–134.

Seegmiller, J. E. (1972). Lesch-Nyhan syndrome and the X-linked uric acidurias. *Hospital Practice, 7,* 79–90.

*Shukla, S., & Albin, R. W. (1996). Effects of extinction alone and extinction plus functional communication training on covariation of problem behaviors. *Journal of Applied Behavior Analysis, 29,* 565–568.

*Sigafoos, J., & Kerr, M. (1994). Provision of leisure activities for the reduction of challenging behavior. *Behavioral Interventions, 9,* 43–53.

*Sigafoos, J., & Meikle, B. (1996). Functional communication training for the treatment of multiply determined challenging behavior in two boys with autism. *Behavior Modification, 20,* 60–84.

*Sigafoos, J., Penned, D., & Versluis, J. (1996). Naturalistic assessment leading to effective treatment of self-injury in a young boy with multiple disabilities. *Education and Treatment of Children, 19,* 101–123.

Singer, G. H. S., Singer, J., & Horner, R. H. (1987). Using pretask requests to increase the probability of compliance for students with severe disabilities. *Journal of The Association for Persons With Severe Handicaps, 12,* 287–291.

Skinner, B. F. (1974). *About behaviorism.* New York: Vintage.

*Slifer, K. J., Ivancic, M. T., Parrish, J. M., Page, T. J., & Burgio, L. D. (1986). Assessment and treatment of multiple behavior problems exhibited by a profoundly retarded adolescent. *Journal of Behavior Therapy and Experimental Psychiatry, 17,* 203–213.

Smith, M. D. (1985). Managing the aggressive and self-injurious behavior of adults disabled by autism. *Journal of The Association for Persons With Severe Handicaps, 10,* 228–232.

Smith, M. D. (1986). Use of similar sensory stimuli in the community-based treatment of self-stimulatory behavior in an adult disabled by autism. *Journal of Behavior Therapy and Experimental Psychiatry, 17,* 121–125.

Smith, M. D. (1990). *Autism and life in the community.* Baltimore: Paul H. Brookes.

*Smith, M. D., & Coleman, D. (1986). Managing the behavior of adults with autism in the job setting. *Journal of Autism and Developmental Disorders, 16,* 145–154.

*Smith, R. G., Iwata, B. A., Vollmer, T. R., & Zarcone, J. R. (1993). Experimental analysis and treatment of multiply controlled self-injury. *Journal of Applied Behavior Analysis, 26,* 183–196.

Snell, M. E. (Ed.). (1993). *Instruction of students with disabilities* (4th ed.). New York: Merrill.

Sovner, R. (1989). The use of valproate in the treatment of mentally retarded persons with typical and atypical bipolar disorders. *Journal of Clinical Psychiatry, 50* (Suppl. 3), 40–43.

*Sprague, J., Holland, K., & Thomas, K. (1997). The effect of noncontingent sensory reinforcement, contingent sensory reinforcement, and response blocking on stereotypical and self-injurious behavior. *Research in Developmental Disabilities, 18,* 61–77.

*Sprague, J. R., & Horner, R. H. (1992). Covariation within functional response classes: Implications for treatment of severe problem behavior. *Journal of Applied Behavior Analysis, 25,* 735–745.

*Steed, S. E., Bigelow, K. M., Huynen, K. B., & Lutzker, J. R. (1995). The effects of planned activities training, low demand schedule, and reinforcement sampling on adults with developmental disabilities who exhibit challenging behaviors. *Journal of Developmental and Physical Disabilities, 7*, 303–316.

*Steege, M. W., Wacker, D. P., Berg, W. K., Cigrand, K. K., & Cooper, L. J. (1989). The use of behavioral assessment to prescribe and evaluate treatments for severely handicapped children. *Journal of Applied Behavior Analysis, 22*, 23–33.

*Steege, M. W., Wacker, D. P., Cigrand, K. C., Berg, W. K., Novak, C. G., Reimers, T. M., Sasso, G. M., & DeRaad, A. (1990). Use of negative reinforcement in the treatment of self-injurious behavior. *Journal of Applied Behavior Analysis, 23*, 459–467.

Stokes, T. F., & Baer, D. M. (1977). An implicit technology of generalization. *Journal of Applied Behavior Analysis, 10*, 349–367.

Sturmey, P. (1994). Assessing the functions of aberrant behaviors: A review of psychometric instruments. *Journal of Autism and Developmental Disorders, 24*, 293–304.

*Taylor, C. R., & Chamove, A. S. (1986). Vibratory and visual stimulation reduces self-injury. *Australia and New Zealand Journal of Developmental Disabilities, 12*, 243–248.

Taylor, J. C., & Carr, E. G. (1992). Severe problem behaviors related to social interaction. I: Attention seeking and social avoidance. *Behavior Modification, 16*, 305–335.

Taylor-Greene, S., Brown, D., Nelson, L., Longton, J., Gassman, T., Cohen, J., Swartz, J., Horner, R. H., Sugai, G., & Hall, S. (1997). School-wide behavioral support: Starting the year off right. *Journal of Behavioral Education, 7*, 99–112.

Thompson, T., Hackenberg, T., & Schaal, D. (1991). Pharmacological treatments for behavior problems in developmental disabilities. In U.S. Department of Health and Human Services, *Treatment of destructive behaviors in persons with developmental disabilities* (NIH Publication No. 91-2410, pp. 343–510). Washington, DC: National Institutes of Health.

Tifft, S. (1996, March). *True life testimony.* Paper presented at the Positive Support Planning Workshop, Eugene, OR.

Touchette, P. E., MacDonald, R. F., & Langer, S. N. (1985). A scatter plot for identifying stimulus control of problem behavior. *Journal of Applied Behavior Analysis, 18*, 343–351.

Turnbull, A. P. (1988). The challenge of providing comprehensive support to families. *Education and Training in Mental Retardation, 23*, 261–272.

Turnbull, A. P., Friesen, B. J., & Ramirez, C. (1998). Participatory Action Research as a model of conducting family research. *Journal of The Association for Persons With Severe Handicaps, 23*, 178–188.

Turnbull, A. P., & Ruef, M. (1996). Family perspectives on problem behavior. *Mental Retardation, 34*, 280–293.

Turnbull, A. P., & Ruef, M. (1997). Family perspectives on inclusive lifestyle issues for people with problem behavior. *Exceptional Children, 63,* 211–227.

Turnbull, A. P., & Turnbull, H. R. (1996). Group action planning as a strategy for providing comprehensive family support. In L. K. Koegel, R. L. Koegel, & G. Dunlap (Eds.), *Positive behavior support: Including people with difficult behavior in the community* (pp. 99–114). Baltimore: Paul H. Brookes.

*Umbreit, J., & Blair, K. S. (1996). The effects of preference, choice, and attention on problem behavior at school. *Education and Training in Mental Retardation, 31,* 151–161.

*Underwood, L. A., Figueroa, R. G., Thyer, B. A., & Nzeocha, A. (1989). Interruption and DRI in the treatment of self-injurious behavior among mentally retarded and autistic self-restrainers. *Behavior Modification, 13,* 471–481.

Vandercook, T., York, J., & Forest, M. (1989). The McGill action planning systems (MAPS): A strategy for building the vision. *Journal of The Association for Persons With Severe Handicaps, 14,* 205–215.

Vaughn, B., & Horner, R. H. (1997). Identifying instructional tasks that occasion problem behaviors and assessing the effects of student versus teacher choice among these tasks. *Journal of Applied Behavior Analysis, 30,* 299–312.

Virginia Institute of Developmental Disabilities. (1996). *Why Jason behaves that way and what to do about it: A dialogue about problem behaviors and positive support for family members and friends* [Booklet]. Richmond, VA: Author.

Vollmer, T. R., & Iwata, B. A. (1992). Differential reinforcement as treatment for behavior disorders: Procedural and functional variations. *Research in Developmental Disabilities, 13,* 393–417.

*Vollmer, T. R., Iwata, B. A., Smith, R. G., & Rodgers, T. A. (1992). Reduction of multiple aberrant behaviors and concurrent development of self-care skills with differential reinforcement. *Research in Developmental Disabilities, 13,* 287–299.

*Vollmer, T. R., Iwata, B. A., Zarcone, J. R., Smith, R. G., & Mazaleski, J. L. (1993). The role of attention in the treatment of attention-maintained self-injurious behavior: Noncontingent reinforcement and differential reinforcement of other behavior. *Journal of Applied Behavior Analysis, 26,* 9–21.

*Vollmer, T. R., Marcus, B. A., & LeBlanc, L. (1994). Treatment of self-injury and hand mouthing following inconclusive functional analyses. *Journal of Applied Behavior Analysis, 27,* 331–344.

*Vollmer, T. R., Marcus, B. A., & Ringdahl, J. E. (1995). Noncontingent escape as treatment for self-injurious behavior maintained by negative reinforcement. *Journal of Applied Behavior Analysis, 28,* 15–26.

Wacker, D. P., Steege, M. W., Northup, J., Sasso, G., Berg, W., Reimers, T., Cooper, L., Cigrand, K., & Donn, L. (1990). A component analysis of functional communication training across three topographies of severe behavior problems. *Journal of Applied Behavior Analysis, 23,* 417–429.

Wheeler, J. J. (1996). The use of interactive focus groups to aid in the identification of perceived service and support delivery needs of persons with developmental disabilities and their families. *Education and Training in Mental Retardation and Developmental Disabilities, 31,* 294–303.

White, C., Lakin, K., Bruininks, R., & Li, X. (1991). *Persons with mental retardation and related conditions in state-operated residential facilities: Year ending June 30, 1989 with longitudinal trends from 1950–1989.* Minneapolis: University of Minnesota, Center for Residential and Community Services, Institute on Community Integration.

Wiesler, N. A., Hanson, R. H., Chamberlain, T. P., & Thompson, T. (1985). Functional taxonomy of stereotypic and self-injurious behavior. *Mental Retardation, 23,* 230–234.

Willemsen-Swinkels, S. H. N., Buitelaar, J. K., Nijhof, G. J., & van Engeland, H. (1995). Failure of naltrexone hydrochloride to reduce self-injurious and autistic behavior in mentally retarded adults. *Archives of General Psychiatry, 52,* 766–773.

*Winterling, V., Dunlap, G., & O'Neill, R. E. (1987). The influence of task variation on the aberrant behaviors of autistic students. *Education and Treatment of Children, 10,* 105–119.

Wolery, M., & Ezell, H. K. (1993). Subject descriptions and single subject research. *Journal of Learning Disabilities, 26,* 642–647.

Wolf, M. M. (1978). Social validity: The case for subjective measurement, or how applied behavior analysis is finding its heart. *Journal of Applied Behavior Analysis, 11,* 203–214.

*Zarcone, J. R., Iwata, B. A., Mazaleski, J. L., & Smith, R. G. (1994). Momentum and extinction effects on self-injurious escape behavior and noncompliance. *Journal of Applied Behavior Analysis, 27,* 649–658.

*Zarcone, J. R., Iwata, B. A., Smith, R. G., Mazaleski, J. L., & Lerman, D. C. (1994). Reemergence and extinction of self-injurious escape behavior during stimulus (instructional) fading. *Journal of Applied Behavior Analysis, 27,* 307–316.

*Zarcone, J. R., Iwata, B. A., Vollmer, T. R., Jagtiani, S., Smith, R. G., & Mazaleski, J. L. (1993). Extinction of self-injurious escape behavior with and without instructional fading. *Journal of Applied Behavior Analysis, 26,* 353–360.

Zeiler, M. D. (1970). Other behavior: Consequences of reinforcing not responding. *Journal of Psychology, 74,* 149–155.